POETIC WHISPERS

Poetic Whispers from the Cauldron of the Otherworld

by Shonagh Home

Published by Logosophia, LLC
Asheville, North Carolina
https://logosophiabooks.com

POETIC WHISPERS FROM THE CAULDRON OF THE OTHERWORLD

Library of Congress Cataloging-in-Publication Data:

Cover Artist: Edmund Dulac, Annabel Lee, 1912
Cover design and interior layout by Susan Yost

ISBN: 979-8-9890902-1-1

For the Sidhe folk

And for my beautiful daughters,

Lovingly graced by the Shining Ones.

This book is a beautiful balance of treats and nourishment for both the analytical left brain and the lyrical right brain. Shonagh builds a container from historical research of Faery lore that perfectly holds the magic of the poetic transmissions. Be warned, this magic is contagious! After reading a while you may find yourself speaking in rhyme as well:

In these pages magic lies
Deep and true and pure and wide
Dive within, you'll be pleased
With the blessings you'll receive...

– Lindsey Swope, Executive Director, Gaian Fairy Congress

A charmingly eloquent journey into the heartland of the Sidhe, the fairy realms. Infused with the fiery fairy power of inspiration, Shonagh's poetry shines a light on the spiritual reality of life, as she engages with the nature beings in shamanic states of super-awareness. We can share in the wise counsel offered. The messages have universal resonance and they encourage us to follow a sensitive path and protect our mother planet.

– Alanna Moore, Australian-Irish Geomancer and Author

Shonagh's writing is enchanted and mystical and will leave the reader inspired. She introduces us to the beauty of Celtic folklore and takes us on a traverse through the magical world of the Faerie realm. The wisdom of the mushroom teachers comes through her poetry with breathtaking clarity to share their message with us. Shonagh's personal story reveals the inner guidance that led her to a place of mystery and beauty, grounded in the realty of the everyday world that surrounds us with its industrial and technological challenges. She invites us in a powerful voice to return to the wisdom of Nature, reestablish right relationship, and live in harmony with Life. To be immersed in the world Shonagh shares with us is a rare gift. Thank you!

– Dr. Tom Garcia, Psychedelic Guide and Integration Coach

Strung on branches so stalwart and well-researched as to call the ancient oak to mind, a lacey web of magical messages has been delivered into the sensitive hands of Mushroom's Apprentice, Shonagh Home. What a blessing to have been given opportunity to be included in the sharing! Human kind would do well to open hearts and minds to the guidance of these wise elders of forest, field and stream.

– Gaelen Billingsley LMFT

Poetic Whispers starts with a generous and very readable introduction to the *Three Cauldrons Of Poesy*. I find that to be one of the best tools for us to enter the realm that Shonagh's book guides us through. Without that, there may be no intimate understanding of what poetry is. Poetic Whispers is beyond just a poetry book, Shonagh uses poetry to prompt and guide us. Her perceptive poetry invites us to join her in that sensory realm that has no words. To me, that's how a writer can nourish us. Thank you for this sharing, Shonagh Home.

– John Willmott of Nature Folklore

Shonagh's psilocybin inspired poetry transmissions are enchanting, lyrical, and transformative, and I love the meta-message of support from the unseen Faerie worlds, the promise of a return to the Garden, and the feeling you get about the potential and magic of multidimensional trance states and poetic expression. What I also love about this book is the rich historical foundation of Celtic Lore, with its banshees, bards and cauldrons, which illuminates how important a place Poetry holds for one who is on an archetypal journey—as are we all, whether we know it or not. While the psychedelic renaissance we are currently experiencing has put much of the emphasis on the measurable and clinical healing of crises like trauma and depression, it is through accessing one's poetic imagination that one connects with Nature in all its seen and unseen glory, including the Self-Nature, and that's where true healing happens.

– Lakshmi Narayan, Cofounder of Awake.net,
Creative Director for AwakeMedia.com

"O Poets! Shamans of the word! When will you recover the trance-like rhythms, the subliminal imagery, the haunting sense of possession, the power, inflection and enunciation to affect the vision?

Shamanize! Shamanize!"

        – *Birth of a Poet* by William Everson

TABLE OF CONTENTS

Acknowledgements

I am indebted to my beloved friend, 'Leif', who initiated me into the shimmering realms of the mushroom, and opened my heart to the mossy green magic of an ancient forest. You have changed my life utterly, and this book wouldn't have happened without you.

To the many dear people with whom I've shared my poetry over the years, your touching responses and encouragement have given me the courage to share beyond my kitchen table these lyrical transmissions.

To my publishers, Steve and Krys Crimi, I thank you from my heart for your enthusiastic support of my writing. This has meant the world to me and I cherish both of you.

And to my dearly loved Sidhe—*Is leatsa mo chladaí, mo chairde...*

The Fairie Queen by Jessie M Meek 1928.

As psilocybin mushrooms are often called, 'magic mushrooms', this book is just one of many windows into how wondrous that magic can be, and how that magic can be brought into this world.

Having read through this book in the process of writing and compiling all the material, it occurred to me that this is a magical manual of sorts. The poetry enchants and the weave of the words has the power to penetrate through our social programming to touch that place of pure imagination and possibility within. In so doing, it animates our creativity, intuition and inspiration, and that is essential nourishment for the spirit of magic to flourish.

The poems in this book are poetic transmissions from the realm of Faerie, accessed through the portal of the mushroom and through alpha and theta states. The transmissions are not actual Faerie tales of course, but I have found in the responses of those who've listened to me read them aloud that they have a similar enchanting effect to the old poetic Faerie tales that Rudolf Steiner spoke of in a lecture he gave in 1908, now titled, 'The Poetry and Meaning of Fairy Tales.' Steiner mentions the 'folk soul', and it is that very folk soul that I have touched in these last dozen years of traversing the mushroom realms and exploring my own cultural roots. Steiner stated,

> ...it is just this poetic enchantment that causes one to feel strongly about fairy tales; studying them or trying to explain them with one's own ideas must surely destroy their fresh spontaneity, yes, even the whole effect of the tales. We often hear it said quite rightly that explanations and commentaries of poetry spoil the immediate, lively, artistic impression that a poem should give us; we want it to affect us simply on its own. All the more should this apply to the infinitely subtle and bewitching quality of the poetic tales arising from the deep, almost bottomless springs of the folk soul or from single human hearts. They flow out in such an original way that intruding our own strong judgment would seem like tearing a flower to pieces.

We are living in an ever-burgeoning synthetic, sterile world that seeks to ensure we are divorced not only from Nature and her cycles but also from our respective ancestral myths and mystical connections to the unseen realms that have nurtured the folk spirit our people once held dear. I remember a retreat client who excitedly told me she'd purchased several old books on the Faerie from a library that was purging all such books from its collection. So many libraries around the U.S. have done this these past few years and the replacement books featured for children are devoid of the wonder and mystical depth those tales invoke.

In one of his lectures, Steiner said, "Fairy tales and sagas are comparable to a good angel, granted human beings as a companion from birth on their life's wanderings, to be a trustworthy comrade throughout— offering comradeship, and making life inwardly into a truly ensouled fairy tale!"

Dr Helmut von Kugelgen, who taught at the original Waldorf school in Stuttgart, wrote, "Each person needs a field of activity for his inner life, for his willing, feeling, and finally for his thinking soul. The child needs this field of activity for the strength of his soul as does each adult. If I do not present the child with the images of the language of the fairy tales, then the contents of his soul will be supplied by the idle talk of the alley. Car makes and money concerns; trivial, unimaginative bits of everyday conversation will rule the field of his soul, resulting in a field filled with weeds."[1]

Austrian Anthroposophist and writer, Frederick Hiebel, wrote, "In the art and fantasy of fairy tales lies a very deep wisdom which has power to awaken children from the sleep of ordinary life. Forces of healing are also hidden in each fairy tale. The most important effect of the fairy tale is that they stimulate the feeling that man is a being of development, of struggle, of metamorphosis, and that behind all the adverse forces of giants and dwarfs, witches and demons there lies the good world of the true genius of man."[2]

It is my hope that the poetic messages throughout this book will stimulate that true genius that each and every one of us holds. And so, this book is a kind of Faerie tale for grown-ups and I assure you the Faerie are as real as the book you hold in your hand, and magic is not only real, you are steeped in it day and night. Magic is the electromagnetic field that all of life is bathed in, and we have the ability to create an intentioned charge via thought, words and action, that can materialize over time in a myriad of ways. We can cultivate connection to the fathomless generosity of the unseen intelligences of Nature, and that will serve not only to change our life as we know it but will also infuse the larger world with a magic this Earth hasn't tasted for who knows how long.

Take your time with the poems. If you read them more than once you'll receive the meaning more deeply. If a transmission speaks to you personally, consider that as not merely a coincidence. The mystery is ingenious in the infinite ways it knows to get a specific message across. The use of poetry to deliver that message is especially productive. I have been graced, and I sincerely share that grace with you through these pages.

The Magic Circle, John William Waterhouse, 1886. (Tate, London.)

Mushrooms, Cauldrons and Poetry

Tá sé i nDán—(def.) It is fated, but literally "it is in a poem." Poetry and prophecy were one and the same in pre-Norman Ireland.

– Seán Pádraig O'Donoghue

In the words of Lady Wilde (Oscar Wilde's mother), "...for music and poetry are fairy gifts, and the possessors of them show kinship to the spirit race—therefore they are watched over by the spirit of life, which is prophecy and inspiration..."

Poetry could almost be thought of as its own unique language, and one that holds a palpable magic. Is it any wonder that many spells are cast poetically? There is something within us that seems to recognize the difference in quality between a piece of poetry and the common parlance, and we adjust our receptiveness accordingly. As a grateful recipient of poetic transmissions via the portal of the mushroom I have come to see how poetry itself is a powerful portal that delivers an actual experience, going beyond intellect to a state of feeling, often deep and profound.

Barbara Tedlock, PhD, author of *The Woman in the Shaman's Body* wrote: "Shamans are seers, oracles, and oral poets and their artistic language creates a healing path for their patients."[3] I live in the spirit of those words as I extend my hand to the forest teachers who have been engaging and inspiring me in profound ways since my twelve months of ritual mushroom journeys at the age of forty-eight. The first six of those journeys took place in the dark of night in the mossy temple of the Olympic National Rainforest in Washington State. There, I underwent a kind of 'soul's training' where I crossed the portal each month and opened myself as initiate to the ancient teachers found within the mushroom realms. This mysterious fungal sacrament could be likened to a magical college that has long been used by adepts and initiates through the ages as a doorway into secret knowledge and timeless wisdom. What I have touched into is as old as the hills and long practiced by medicine folk, oracles, seers, priests and priestesses through the ages.

I recently read a post by herbalist, writer and teacher, Seán Pádraig O'Donoghue, who referenced herbalist Stephen Buhner's term for psychedelic plants and fungi as 'neurognostic', and shared that Buhner spoke of them as *Elders of Gaia*. 'Elders of Gaia!' How perfect is that? I wholeheartedly concur. Through my own dedicated engagement with them I have accessed an inner doorway through which counsel in the form of poetic messages flows from a variety of spirit beings, most commonly a group who refer to themselves as *The Shining Ones you Call the Sidhe*, (shee). There is a sense when they come through of being with old friends for whom I feel a longing to return and yet no actual memory of what past we might have shared through the ages. In this life, they serve as guides and teachers as I traverse the course of my earthly incarnation. After receiving their poetic messages, whether via the mushroom or in my waking state, I am always filled with humbled gratitude and appreciation for the gift of their counsel.

When I am called to the mushroom, I enter into a type of shamanic practice called 'mediumship', where our spirits converge and information is exchanged. This is a high trance state that men and women over the ages have practiced in many forms, using plants, fungi, sound, dance, incubation, and other practices to bring about an altered state of being. Under the veil of the mushroom my voice changes markedly and I speak in poetic prose as different intelligences express through me. I enter this state alone in quiet darkness, where I can be fully present to the telepathic communication.

The poetry within this book represents my personal journey over the past twelve years, moving from a dark night of the soul to a profound connection with Nature intelligences that have been guiding me ever since. These beings proffer wisdom and magical knowledge, and they bring a winking humor into their wordplay. The natural world is very much alive and accessible if we can break the spell of our modern mental programming. We must shift our state of awareness to a place of receptivity to the subtle layers of this world. I have found that through trance states ranging from alpha—such as a long walk, run or daydreaming—to theta, as in a mushroom journey or semi-conscious dream state, I am able to unlock that inner door and receive poetic transmissions. It is in these states where I find myself in conversation with intelligences that otherwise go relatively undetected in my daily waking state.

That said, my sensitivity to these subtle intelligences has developed markedly over my years of engagement with the mushroom, which has changed my brain over time to where my natural psychic abilities have been enhanced. In addition, having lived in a haunted house in my adolescence, I became quite skilled out of necessity in 'feeling' a room or environment. This is an innate ability we all possess though it is often not developed beyond a basic sixth sense. It's there nevertheless, and it can be cultivated through various practices.

A few years into my mushroom explorations I travelled to Scotland to tour the Outer Hebrides with author, researcher and speaker, Freddy Silva. In a small stone circle on the Isle of Lewis, I encountered a tall male spirit who handed me a golden orb that I placed in the center of my chest. After that occurrence I had poetry flowing through me at each site we visited and I dictated the messages into my digital recorder, which thankfully, I'd brought with me. A later message on that tour asked me to think of the golden orb as a cauldron I was to work with alchemically.

Callanish, Isle of Lewis.

The cauldron has powerful associations for the Celts. Many centuries ago it was an essential and valuable container for the ancient Celts, who used it for brewing, bathing and transporting water. The cauldron also had mystical associations and was thought to hold magical and alchemical properties. One easily observed how anything put into a cauldron came out utterly changed. When the fire was lit below it, water began to simmer, bubble and boil and ingredients changed in shape and flavor. The cauldron linked the elements of water and fire, and the goddess, Brighid, muse of poets, oversaw both.

A cauldron traditionally rests on three legs, and the number three has tremendous significance in Celtic art and myth. As well, both the cauldron and the number three were highly symbolic to the poet initiates of old Ireland. There were three cauldrons of incubation that symbolized the levels of bardic training. *Coire Goiriath* (Cauldron of Warming or Incubation), symbolized the first stage of apprenticeship where the poet initiates learned the basic skills of their art. *Coire Ermae* (Cauldron of Motion), represented the heart-center of the chest where emotions were woven with life experience and teachings that the poets "stewed," on to produce poetry of depth and beauty. The third cauldron was the *Coire Sofhis* (Cauldron of Wisdom), where illumination was found through the culmination of the training. This cauldron incubated the highest level of magical training, wisdom, and divine knowledge, producing a poet on the level of a Taliesin or Amergin.

Christopher Scott Thompson, author of *A God Who Makes Fire*, writes of a text that was written by a high-ranking Irish seer poet in the 7th century who went by the name of Amergin. By then, Christianity had been established for a few centuries, and though the druids were still present, their influence had diminished greatly to where they ranked beneath the *fili*. The text is titled, *Cauldron of Poesy*, and it speaks to the three inner cauldrons. There are a few different translations and interpretations and according to Thompson, they are all likely correct. Erynn Rowan Laurie translated this writing in the 90s and interprets it as a mystical text, connecting the three cauldrons to chakra centers in the body. Scholars, Liam Breatnach and PL Henry have differing interpretations from that of Laurie's, determining that the poem is speaking metaphorically to the training of the seer poets as I shared above.

An excerpt from the poem states,

> In some it is on its side, in some on its lips, in some on its back,
> On its lips in the foolish, on its side in the talented,
> and upright in the master poet.

Later in the text the poet writes:

> What then is the origin of poetic art and all of knowledge in general? That is not difficult to answer. Three cauldrons are generated inside each person who has wisdom—the Cauldron of Incubation, the Cauldron of Motion and the Cauldron of Wisdom.
>
> The Cauldron of Incubation is upright from the moment it is generated. It dispenses wisdom to people as they study in youth.
>
> The Cauldron of Motion, however, magnifies a person after it is turned upright.
>
> It is on its side when first generated.
>
> The Cauldron of Wisdom is upside-down when generated. If this cauldron can be turned, it distributes the wisdom of every art there is.
>
> The Cauldron of Motion, then, is upside-down in ignorant people. It is on its side in mere practitioners of poetry, but it is upright in the master poets who are like great streams of wisdom. So it is that not everyone has the cauldron upright during the early years of practicing his art, for it must be turned upright by sorrow or joy.

The poet speaks to the locations of the cauldrons in the body, which identify specific stored energies and how they can be developed by training. The Cauldron of Incubation is located in the *boinn*, Gaelic for the belly, and this is identical to the *dantien* of Traditional Chinese Medicine, the seat of chi which is located three finger widths below the navel. The poets would speak of being 'pregnant' (incubated) with poetry, referring to this dynamic energy center. The Cauldron of Motion (also known as Vocation), is located in the heart center or heart chakra area where feeling is experienced. The Cauldron of Wisdom is located between the brows where the pineal gland or third eye is found. One's responses to various life experiences, whether joy or sorrow, will cause the cauldrons to turn.

Where does this inner cauldron derive its power? Thompson writes,

> "So, what our text is telling us here is that the cauldron's power or essence derives from the same fundamental energies of which both the world and the self are made. Just like the *duilean* (elements) themselves, the cauldron is both within the individual person (in the physical body and in the psyche) and in the spiritual landscape of the divine realm."[4]

The manuscript of the *Bretha Nemed* cited three colors of poetry or the *dath an ai,* which are black, white and speckled. White is for poetry of praise, and the high-ranking poets were hired to write poems of glowing praise for the kings who employed them. Black poetry was satire, and woe be to the king or other individual of rank who crossed the *fili* poets, for they would be satirized, thereby greatly reduced in the eyes of their peers. Speckled poetry was that of warning to anyone who was skating on thin ice with an influential poet who could do great social damage with their golden tongue.

'Entrance stone', Newgrange, circa 3200 BC.

The triskelion is a symbol of triplicity composed of three spirals joined at the center. It's found in Celtic carving, metalwork, weaving and more. It was carved into the walls of Newgrange long before the Celts arrived and they embraced its design and incorporated it widely. The symbol of three features prominently in myth and there are numerous triads beginning with the three women who represent Ireland herself—Ériu, Banba, and Fódla. The three gods of craftsmanship were Credne, Goibniu and Luchta. The Dagda of the Tuatha De Danaan had a daughter, the goddess, Brighid, who is three deities in one. She has been shown as three sisters, all with the name Brighid, each sister overseeing a particular art—smithcraft, poetry and healing. Brighid had three sons, Brian, Iuchar and Uar. In Ireland the gods, ancestors and land spirits are called the Na Trí Naomh—'the sacred three', and the three realms are land, sea and sky. The number three also has magical and ritualistic associations—spells, phrases and actions repeated three times, three drops of a ritual brew, etc.

In his book, *Time Stands Still: New Light on Megalithic Science*, Keith Critchlow writes, "There is also evidence that the druid oral tradition was taught in triads, that is in short poems with a content of three elements. In the case of the ancient Welsh triads the letters of the alphabet were themselves composed of three basic elements."[5]

On that subject there is a collection of 256 Old Irish poems that offer practical, common-sense advice known as *The Triads of Ireland* or *Trecheng Breth Féne*, meaning 'triple judgments of the freemen'. These poems consist of a particular theme with three concise expressions of it and cover such topics as behavior, Nature, law, custom, geography and more. One such example says, "Three rude ones of the world: a youngster mocking an old man, a healthy person mocking an invalid, a wise man mocking a fool." Artist, horticulturist and bard, Olivia Wylie, created a beautiful illustrated book on these triads titled, *The Triads of Ireland: An Illustrated Collection*. I highly recommend availing yourself of all three of her majestic books that feature Irish cultural heritage in its fullness.

The cauldron is a symbol of alchemy, magic, containment, fertility, germination, transmutation, abundance, death and regeneration, and poetic inspiration. It played a major role in Celtic lore. There was the cauldron of the Daghda, which was known as the Cauldron of Plenty. This was one of the four treasures of the Tuatha Dé Danann and it was an ever-constant source of sustenance for his people. His cauldron never emptied, illuminating his connection to agriculture and fertility.

What is the ever-full cauldron? Answer. A Cauldron which should be always kept on the fire for every party that should arrive...which returns in a perfect state whatever is put into it, while every other cauldron would dissolve it...

– Senchas Mor

Another example is the cauldron of Bran the Blessed, the high king of the Island of the Mighty. This cauldron brought the dead back to life and conferred rejuvenation and rebirth to all who partook from it.

Probably the most famous myth involving a cauldron is that of the Welsh goddess, Cerridwen, who was the powerful muse of the poets, and the formidable initiator of the poet, Taliesin, whose name means 'radiant brow'. Her cauldron was located in the underworld, the realm of Annwn. In this story she brews a magical potion for her unfortunate son, Afagddu (Morfran). The brew is called, 'Awen', which translates to 'flowing spirit' or 'inspiration', and it takes a year and a day to potentize. Just three drops from the cauldron's brew would bestow a profound rebirth, conferring knowledge, wisdom and poetic inspiration to anyone who drank from it. If more than three drops of the cauldron's brew were ingested, death would be the result. Though the brew was intended for Afagddu, it was not to be. Cerridwen had employed a young boy, Gwion Bach, to stir the brew and the fire beneath was tended by a blind man named Morda.

In Taliesin's poem, *The Chair of Cerridwen*, the Goddess declares,

When all the Chairs are compared
Mine is pre-eminent.

My Chair, my Cauldron, my Laws.
My searching speech gives them constancy.
I am initiate of the court of Don...

We have here a goddess who knows full well her power and place in the realm. Well, before the brew could be given to Afagddu, it splashed onto Gwion's hand and he immediately put his thumb into his mouth to quell the pain. As a result, he swallowed three drops of the magical brew and was instantly transformed from child to one imbued with the wisdom of the ages. Anticipating Cerridwen's rage, he fled. A chase ensued where both Cerridwen and Gwion shapeshifted into various animals and birds. Cerridwen finally consumed him and nine months later birthed Gwion as the legendary poet, Taliesin.

We see here that the contents of the cauldron are magical and the ingestion of those contents—in the proper dose—will influence the initiate in such a way that he/she will never be the same. Rather, the initiate will be permanently enriched by the effects of the brew, forever possessing knowledge, wisdom and poetic eloquence.

Gundestrup Celtic Cauldron, circa 150 BC, Denmark.

The flames beneath Cerridwen's cauldron of poetic inspiration were stoked by the breath of nine maidens. That is strikingly similar to Greek mythology with the nine muses. And just as three drops of Cerridwen's brew conferred poetic brilliance, three of the Greek muses represented specific forms of poetry. Calliope represented epic poetry, Erato represented love poetry, and Polyrhythmia, sacred poetry. In Celtic myth we have the story of the nine hazel trees whose nuts were equated with wisdom and poetic inspiration. These trees grew around a sacred pool and when their hazelnuts dropped into the water, they were eaten by the salmon that became imbued with their mystical gifts, and so the salmon was sacred to the Druids for its wisdom and power.

The early Irish poets believed that the gift of poetry was given next to the water, which was thought to be the entrance to the Otherworld. As well, *Imbas,* poetic inspiration, was said to be found in plants growing by the River Boyne, which could indicate the ritual use of certain mushrooms such as the Amanita muscaria.

A famous Celtic myth tells of the Salmon of Knowledge that swam in the Well of Segais, eating the magical hazelnuts that fell into the water. The elder poet, Finegas, lived by it for seven years, hoping to catch the salmon. It had been prophesied that whoever was the first to eat the Salmon of Knowledge would have the wisdom of the ages. When the younger Fionn came to him as apprentice the Salmon of Knowledge was finally caught, and Finegas instructed Fionn to cook it but not ingest it. In cooking the salmon Fionn burned his thumb on the hot juices, and like Gwion, put it into his mouth to cool the burn. As soon as Finegas beheld Fionn, he no longer saw the eyes of a young man, for Fionn now had the eyes of the sage. In the story Finegas tells him to eat the salmon and offers him his blessing. Fionn later learns from Finegas the three things that make a poet, which are Fire of Song, Light of Knowledge and the Art of Extempore Recitation, (meaning to speak without preparation). Young Fionn later went on to become Fionn MacCumhail, one of the greatest heroes in Irish mythology. His magic thumb gave him knowledge any time he was in need of it, conferring on him the gifts of poetic divination and legendary skill as a war leader.

People of the ancient world regarded poetry as a divine gift of grace from the gods. In the British Isles, an esteemed class of bards known as the *fili*, were highly trained poets revered for their poetic eloquence and divinatory skills. Their training took place in the cradle of darkness where they could focus without diversion. When their training completed, they were called, 'Ollamh', Doctor of Poetry. The title, "Ollahm" (Olav) indicated the highest degree of an art and was given to the Chief poet. Contrary to the 'struggling artist' today, the poets of this time enjoyed high rank in their society where they were greatly respected. The Order of Bards, Ovates, and Druids describes them as 'custodians of the sacredness of the word'.

The Ollamh carried a beautiful gold branch with bells attached that was shaken upon entering the hall, announcing their arrival and forthcoming recitation. The enchanting sound of the bells hushed the audience and inducted them into the experience, casting a kind of spell that heightened the senses and, coupled with the exquisite prose, touched the very souls of those gathered. The *fili* below the chief were called the *anruth*, and they carried a silver branch, while the remaining lower levels of *fili* carried a bronze branch.

Caitlin Matthews writes,

> This concept of the musical branch seems central to Celtic tradition. The branch was analogous to the branch of the Otherworldly tree which grew in the Blessed Islands of the West on which sat the Birds of Rhiannon. Whoever heard them remained in a timeless state, as do Bran and his Noble Company in the story of Branwen. In 'The Settling of the Manor of Tara,' we read of Trefuilngid Tre-eochair (T. of the Three Keys or Saplings), a great Otherworldly being of titanic size, who comes to Tara bearing in his hands a branch with three fruits upon it: nuts, apples and acorns. This concept of the ever-fertile Otherworldly tree is closely related to the vitality of poetic creation and tradition, which is continually renewed in every generation, passing from master to student.[6]

Birds were sacred to the ancient Celts and seen as keepers of magical knowledge and power, and the Ollahm, who were known for their divinatory skills, wore an impressive cloak made of feathers known as a *tuigen* or bird mantel. It is thought that some of the feathers that composed the cloak came from swans and herons, both of which were sacred to the Celts for their Otherworldly associations. Cormac's *Glossary of Old Irish* word meanings describes a *tuigen* as a "Covering (*tuige*) of birds (*én*, for it is of skins of birds white and many-coloured that the poets' toga is made from their girdle downwards, and of mallards' necks and of their crests from the girdle upwards to their neck."[7] Though referred to as a toga in the glossary, the *tuigen* is thought to have been a cloak and was best described in a story from the *Book of Leinster*, titled, 'The Colloquoy of the Two Sages'. In the story the son of the deceased Ollamh to the king puts on his father's cloak, "And he went and sat down in the Ollave's chair, and took his robe around him. There were three colours of the robe, to wit, a covering of bright birds' feathers in the middle: a showery speckling of Findruine (Tinned Bronze or Electrum) on the lower half outside, and a golden colour on the upper half."[8]

The European and Mediterranean cultures cherished poetic prose and availed themselves of mead, a honey wine known as 'the drink of inspiration'. It was imbibed by the Druids as well as Germanic, Scandinavian and Mediterranean people alike. It was often spiked with other ingredients known to heighten poetic ability. Were they psychoactive? Very probably. The people of these early cultures regularly ingested mead, beer, and other brews in gatherings, and also in ritual and ceremonial practices, where they would be enhanced with additional ingredients. The *Prose Edda* spoke of the Skaldic mead, saying, "whoever drinks from which becomes a poet or a scholar." The *Rigveda* describes Soma-haoma, a ritual psychoactive, in this way, "O juice that is adorned with all poetic thoughts."[9]

That sounds like a little more than just a good glass of wine to me.

Other inspiration-inducing substances include the ethylene gas that emitted from a crevasse beneath the temple of Delphi. The oracles of that temple, seated upon a tripod, inhaled the fumes at certain times of the year, which put them into an ecstatic state, enabling them to channel the deity. In this way they accessed knowledge from the unseen world and brought through prophecy and counsel. Interestingly, their prophesies were delivered poetically in dactylic hexameter, which is a form of meter or rhythmic scheme in poetry. The use of poetry in prophecy was a sign of its divine origin and the two were inextricably linked throughout the ancient world.

In his book, *Drunk the Night Before: An Anatomy of Intoxication*, author, Marty Roth, writes, "People who argue that drugs and drink in the practice of modern art are a parodic reduction are not considering how this practice echoes the origin of poetry in shamanism."[10] The Mazatec shamanic tradition illustrates this in their mushroom rituals where it is understood that the psychoactive mushrooms are a sentient intelligence that communicates information. It is the job of the shaman to bring that communication through in chant or song. Maria Sabina is an eloquent example of this, where she served in ritual as the voice of the mushroom with her poetic chants. The Huichol Indians known as, *Wixárika,* meaning 'healers' or 'prophets', conduct peyote rituals. In these ceremonies the healer sings through the messages from the peyote, which are then shared with the participants.

The use of poetic prose by shamanic folk throughout time shows us a pathway through a kind of magical speech that accesses the unseen world. In fact, it appears that those on the other side of the veil speak in poetic language, which the seer/shaman channels through in song or prose to bring counsel, healing, inspiration and magical knowledge to their people. Invocations are often spoken poetically, as are spells and also curses. Author Caitlin Matthews writes, "...the roots of poetry are inextricably entwined with the mantic arts of invocation, memory, and the inner realms. The high art of poetry as practiced by the *fili*, the master poets, brought them into a similar alignment with the wisdom practiced by the druids."[11]

The recitation of a poem can bring its listeners into a subtle altered state where the consciousness is bathed in the beauty and meaning of the dancing lyrical play of words. The one who recites must be as connected to the poetry as they are to the air they breathe. From that place, the spoken prose affects the very ions in the air and souls are stirred by the vibratory field created in that moment. This is a frequency that is palpably felt in the deepest layers of our being. One can understand how the rhythmic, dancing power of poetically constructed spells has the ability to affect reality.

From the standpoint of our modern mindset, beset by materialist, factory-culture programming since early childhood, this kind of talk is pure nonsense and most people prefer to cleave to their indoctrinated beliefs and so-called opinions they've been programmed to embrace. Yet, there is a mythical layer of existence calling from behind the mist and it doesn't care a fig what the prevailing belief systems of the day dictate, for those beliefs are transitory, while the sublime mystery of Nature is timeless.

With psychedelics so popular today and corporations scrambling to get in the 'game' and monopolize the action as it were, these mystical states of beauty, inspiration and poetry are at risk of being cast aside in favor of a state-approved conventional model that is more concerned with getting people back to work than bringing them in touch with the numinous. A soft light of divine knowing within beckons with the promise of touching a deeper layer of our being, one that offers a profound sense of connection and communion with the greater world and the unseen worlds beyond. Psychedelics or 'entheogens', as they are also called, are a potential pathway to that place of inner knowing. In that place is found the muse, who graciously sings her poetry through in a myriad of ways to cultivate the spark of the Divine found within.

This book is the result of the muse's gift so kindly offered to me through my journeys into the mushroom realms. Today, my path is inspired by the *ban draoi* (dree) and *fili*, the Celtic medicine women and seer poets who held a deep reverence for Nature, the power of the word, and the world of spirit. I serve as a conduit for mystical and practical counsel and magical knowledge. This is, for the most part a solo occupation. Throughout time, many seers and medicine practitioners lived a reclusive life either within the walls of a temple or nunnery, or on the outskirts of the general community.

The Celtic culture had their priestly class known as the Druids, men and women alike, who served as intermediaries between the worlds of the seen and the unseen. They utilized divination, prophecy, healing and magical practices, and were learned in law, botany, music, astronomy, geometry, poetry, myth, and much more. Though the role of seer, medicine man/woman seems to have faded into obscurity, it has not disappeared altogether. Many indigenous cultures still have their medicine folk and there are growing numbers of such people from a multitude of modern cultures who have answered the call and are inspiring others to explore their ancestral roots and native folkways that honored and respected Nature and her cycles. They are the midwives, the herbalists, the folklorists, the poets and storytellers, the mystics, the musicians, the artisans, the organic and biodynamic farmers and others whose inner rhythms are in sync with that of the sovereign queen of Nature.

My intention in sharing this poetry is thus to spark in you, dear reader, a felt sense of the innate magic that lives within and without, and is available if we have ears to hear and eyes to see. I hope to stir your soul's memory of the living mystery, magic and grandeur of Nature that remains ever-present, despite the seduction of technology, industry and the materialist mindset of this current reality construct.

Spend time in Nature. Walk in the woods. Sit by a river. Still your mind and call in the muse...

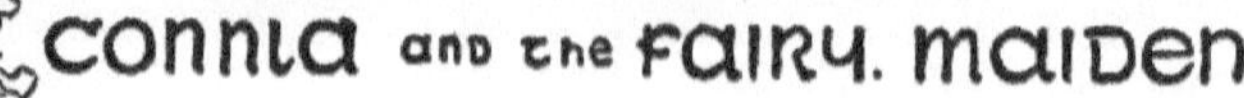

Connla and the Fairy Maiden, illustration from *Childhood Favorites and Fairy Stories*, Various, 1927.

THE FAERIE

The dialogue between our world and the other takes place at the
thresholds and crossing places of both realms, at notable land features,
such as springs, mountains or rivers, or it can happen in dreams, vision
and meditation, when the seer attunes the vision of both realms...
wherein we meet the faery teachers of the seership traditions. As we
enter deeply into these patterns and images, they yield their truth.

– *Celtic Visions* by Caitlin Matthews

In journeying through the mushroom realms over the years I have encountered a variety of different beings. The elemental gnomes have been very prominent and have spoken through me on a number of occasions. They have short bodies, long nose and beard, and very long fingers. The Faerie are always present along with various Nature spirits. Owls and tree spirits make themselves known to me while in trance state, and I've shared a powerful message I received from the trees in the first series of poems. Other beings, celestial in Nature, come in at certain times and there is a specific group of them that I've dubbed, 'the raucous ones', for their brash wit and sense of fun. I don't actually see them clairvoyantly, rather, I know them by their frequency and I can 'feel' how they present to me. Everything alive has a frequency and in both the seen and unseen realms everything has its own frequency signature. When I am in an altered state, I am able to recognize those signatures and I can often do so in my waking state as well.

Cultures around the world have had their 'genius loci' or guardian spirits of place that they respectfully acknowledged. This was an animistic belief that cultures around the world regarded as fact. Early European people were connected to the unseen Nature intelligences that inhabited rocks, trees, water and wells, and also the mountains and hills. Other spirits were believed to be ancestral races that dwelled in specific areas. Celtic lore is rich with stories of these inhabitants whose deeds were memorialized in the great mythology that still captivates today.

The Scandinavian and Germanic people spoke of the *Alfar*, an old Norse word that later morphed into 'elf' in English. The elves were gifted craftsmen and smiths and were often found in the forest. Many people consider the elves to be synonymous with Faeries, and both races have a royal personage of kings and queens. They were synonymous with the land, and the areas they inhabited reflected their characteristics. There are certain areas of the wild that feel welcoming and safe to be in while other areas give off a sense of unwelcome and even danger. Our earlier ancestors viewed that as particular spirits of place, some being friendly and others making it very clear to the traveler to stay away.

There are a variety of Nature spirits that fall under the category of 'Faerie'. In his book, *British Fairy Origins*, Lewis Spence wrote, "The Gaelic Kelts describe all supernaturals as sidhe, which is by no means a designation of the fairies alone, but appears to embrace giants, gruagach-wizards, fairies proper, cailleachs, banshees, and the ghosts of the human dead. All are creatures of a sphere which stands in opposition to the terrestrial, but which has yet certain undoubted associations with it."[12]

The folklore of old Ireland, Scotland and Wales is rich in stories of the Faerie races who were known by different names depending on the area. The people of the Scottish Highlands called them elves, fauns, brownies and Faeries, and also 'the guild folk'. The Faerie of Scotland were said to be ruled by the Queen of Elphame. The old Irish word is *sídheóg* (sheehogue) and fairies are *daoine sidhe* (deenee shee), Faerie people. The word, *sidhe* (shee) (also *síd, síth, síodh, sídh),* means mound or Faerie hill, as the *daoine sidhe* lived below ground and favored mounds, hills and raths for their shimmering abodes. It has long been considered disrespectful to refer to them by their name, 'Faerie', as that could result in bad luck or worse. As well, in magical understanding, to know the name of a spirit is to have power over them. Other terms are used instead such as, 'the good folk', 'the gentry', 'the noble people', 'the Faerie host', the 'seely' (happy or blessed folk), 'the peaceful people', or 'the Lordly Ones', to name a few.

Other Gaelic names are *Bean sí* (banshee), which is a Faerie woman, *Aos sí*, Faeries and inhabitants of Faerie mounds, *An slua sí*, the fairy host and *Sí gaoithe*, a fairy wind or whirlwind. The Sidhe were associated with the wind, which came from a belief that their presence could be felt in a gust of wind. W.B. Yeats wrote that the Irish peasantry said that when the wind flows by, causing leaves and straw to whirl, it was the Faerie, and they would remove their hats respectfully and say, "God bless them." Another belief said when one feels a strong gust of wind it is essential to lie down immediately to avoid being taken by the Faeries. That sentiment and many more like it, is a result of the efforts of the Church to assert authority and order by demonizing the Faerie.

The Faerie are known for making merriment and countless stories tell of troops of Faeries dancing and singing on a moonlit night. In his book, *Irish Folk and Fairy Tales*, Yeats writes, "Their chief occupations are feasting, fighting, and making love and playing the most beautiful music. They traditionally celebrate three specific times of the year, May Eve, Midsummer Eve and November Eve. They can be mischievous and are known for playing pranks." Some are immensely kind and honorable while others of their race are to be cautiously avoided. They demand respect and we must earn theirs. They are easily offended, making their anger known if mistreated or insulted by directing misfortune to those who are careless in their dealings with them.

In his book, *The Fairy Mythology*, Thomas Keightley quotes Thorlacius from the book, *Noget Om Thor og*, by Hans Hammer, saying, "Our heathen forefathers, says Thorlacius, believed, like the Pythagoreans, and the farther back in antiquity, the more firmly, that the whole world was filled with spirits of various kinds to whom they ascribed in general the same nature and properties as the Greeks did to their daemons."[13] These nature spirits have inspired every culture's mythology and folklore. Of Europe's folklore tradition, Jacqueline Simpson, author of *European Mythology* wrote that it "...is concerned with supernatural forces as *real* entities, to be reckoned with in the everyday world, and not just as material for entertaining..."[14]

The Faerie faith of the Celts holds a respectful relationship with these beings that goes back to Neolithic times when ancestors were revered. The Irish Faerie known as the Sidhe are a divine mythical race of beings known as the 'Tuatha De Danann'. They belong to the early mythological cycle of ancient Ireland. Their name roughly translates to 'the tribes or people of the goddess Danu' (or Dana). Danu was the mother of the Celtic gods and was later followed by the goddess, Brighid. It is thought that the Tuatha De Danann determined the yields of agricultural plantings and the milk of cattle, all precious to the people of the land of Éireinn, (Ireland). In myth and folklore they are said to be gods and goddesses, though later Christian-influenced opinion posits that they were fallen angels whose souls were not so dark that they were sent to hell, but rather to Earth to exist in limbo till judgment day decides their fate. They are exquisitely beautiful beings, often depicted with flowing red hair, green eyes and fair skin. They resemble humans and their size can range from medium height to very tall.

The Tuatha De Danann arrived in Ireland and established in the northern islands where they practiced the magical arts. They went to battle with the original inhabitants, the Firbolgs, and successfully purged them from the land. They flourished until the Milesians, the Gaelic sons of Mil, arrived from Spain. An epic battle ensued and the Tuatha De Danann were defeated. After the battle they avenged the sons of Mil by causing the growth of their wheat and the flow of their milk to severely diminish, creating great suffering. A treaty was drawn and the Tuatha De Danann went underground to live beneath the surface, preferring mounds and hills, old forts, caves and lands beneath the waters. Their dwelling places are luminously beautiful palaces known as the Land of Faerie or the Otherworld (*An Saol Eile or* Tír na nÓg). In *The Fairy Faith in Celtic Countries*, W.L. Evans-Wentz shared what the Irish seers told him about the sidhe in the early twentieth century:

> They are described as a race of majestic appearance and marvellous beauty, in form human, yet in nature divine. The highest order of them seems to be a race of beings evolved to a superhuman plane of existence, such as the ancients called gods; and with this opinion, strange as it may seem in this age, all the educated Irish seers with whom I have been privileged to talk agree, though they go further,

and say that these highest Sidhe races still inhabiting Ireland are the ever–young, immortal divine race known to the ancient men of Erin as the Tuatha De Danann.[15]

Countless generations of Celtic people have left offerings of milk, butter and other foods for "the good people," treating them with utmost respect so as to cultivate harmony and not invite misfortune. Evans-Wentz interviewed a priest in West Ireland who was well-versed in Faerie lore who told him, "Whatever milk falls on the ground in milking a cow is taken by the fairies, for fairies need a little milk. Also, after churning, the knife which is run through the butter in drying it must not be scraped clean, for what sticks to it belongs to the fairies. Out of three pounds of butter, for example, an ounce or two would be left for the fairies. I have seen this several times."

And in the town of Tuam, a Mr. John Glynn shared with Evans-Wentz, "Food, after it has been put out at night for the fairies, is not allowed to be eaten afterwards by man or beast, not even by pigs. Such food is said to have no real substance left in it, and to let anything eat it wouldn't be thought of. The underlying idea seems to be that the fairies extract the spiritual essence from food offered to them, leaving behind the grosser elements."[16]

In folklore, the Faerie could be kind or hardhearted. Milk could be curdled or spilled, babies taken, a hapless mortal held in permanent servitude, cattle struck with sudden illness or death, and the lost, purposely misguided. As well, the Faerie could heal the sick or bestow the ability to heal others. They could proffer secrete knowledge and bestow magical gifts, bring sailors safely home and rightly guide lost travelers.

In her most recent book, *Fairy Haunts of Ireland*, geomancer Alanna Moore shares the story of an enchanted rock near Mullaghmore called, Dostann na Briona, the Faerie Rock, which is also known as Doras na Briona, the Portal of Dreams. Alanna writes, "In the past it was common for local people to leave an offering of whiskey or poiteen in a small hole at the top of the rock. A famous incident happened there when a violent storm blew up that risked the lives of the fishermen at sea. Concerned people watching from the shore were amazed to see an ethereal white woman standing in one of the boats. She was only seen by them. The boat survived the tempest, while the others sank. Although they hadn't seen her, the grateful fishermen who arrived safely below the castle knew who to thank. They poured whiskey onto the Fairy Rock in gratitude for the saving of their lives."[17]

There is a story from the mid 1600s of a man accused of witchcraft who told the judge he would take him to the Faerie hill where he was gifted a white powder to heal those in need. The judge regarded him contemptuously but the jury would not convict him. This story was found in an influential book published in 1677 by John Webster titled, *Displaying of Supposed Witchcraft*. That book successfully removed the practice of witchcraft from the Criminal Statute Book. Twenty-four years prior, the author was witness to the man's trial. Webster wrote:

To this I shall only add thus much, that the man was accused for invoking and calling upon evil spirits, and was a very simple and il-literate person to any man's judgment, and had been formerly very poor, but had gotten some pretty little meanes to maintain himself, his wife and diverse small children, by his cures done with this white powder, of which there was sufficient proofs, and the judge asking him how he came by the powder, he told a story to this effect.

That one night before the day was gone, he was going home from his labor being very sad and full of heavy thoughts, not knowing how to get meat and drink for his wife and children. He met a fair woman in fine cloths who asked him why he was so sad and he told her that it was by reason of his poverty, to which she said that if he would follow her counsel she would help him to that which would serve to get him a good living, to which he said he would consent with all his heart so it were not by unlawful ways. She told him that it should not be by any such ways, but by doing of good and curing of sick people and so warning him strictly to meet her there the next night at the same time, she departed from him and he went home. And the next night at the time appointed he duly waited and she (according to her promise) came and told him that it was well he came so duly, otherwise he had missed of that benefit, that she intended to do unto him, and so bade him follow her and not be afraid. There-

upon she led him to a little Hill and she knocked three times, and
the Hill opened and they went in, and came to a fair hall, wherein
was a queen sitting in great state and many people about her, and the
gentlewoman that brought him, presented him to the queen and she
said he was welcome and bid the gentlewoman give him some of the
white powder, and teach him how to use it, which she did, and gave
him a little wood box full of the white powder, and had him give 2 or
3 grains of it to any that were sick, and it would heal them, and so she
brought him forth of the hill, and so they parted. And being asked
by the judge whether the place within the hill, which he called a hall,
were light or dark, he said indifferent, as it is with us in the twilight,
and being asked how he got more powder, he said when he wanted
he went to the hill and knocked three times and said every time, I am
coming, I am coming, whereupon it opened, and he going in was
conducted by the aforesaid woman to the queen, and so had more
powder given him. This was plain and simple story (however it may
be judged of) that he told before the judge, the whole court and the
jury, and there being no proof but what cures he had done to very
many, the jury did acquit him; and I remember the judge said when
all the evidence was heard, that if he were to assign his punishment,
he should be whipped thence to fairy hall, and did seem to judge it
to be a delusion or imposture.[18]

Time in the Land of Faerie is very different than time in our world.
In the world of man, the pace of time is slower, while in the Otherworld,
time moves deceptively and shockingly fast for an unwitting mortal. A
common story in the old folklore is where a mortal has returned from
time spent in the Otherworld, only to discover that a century or more
has passed. He is warned against stepping on the ground, the conse-
quence of which turns him or his allies to dust.

In his book, *The Fairy Mythology*, Thomas Keightly goes into great
detail on the origins of the word 'Faerie', which is too much to cover
here but I do suggest reading his extensively researched book. The word
Faerie hails from the Anglicized version of the old French word, 'fairy"
which derives from 'Fae' or 'fay', originating from the Latin 'fatae',
meaning 'the Fates' (also Latin for 'planets'). Keightly also shares the

plausible theory that goes farther back from that, writing that the word came from the Persian word, *Peri*. The 'Paynim foe' who the Crusaders encountered in Palestine, spoke Arabic, and in the Arabic language there is no 'p', for which the substitute is 'f'. The word 'peri' was pronounced 'feri', and was taken back to Europe by the crusaders and pilgrims who shared the enchanting old tales of Asia. Persia has its own exquisite Faerie stories, which extended outward to the rest of the world.

Of the numerous kinds of Faerie, one well-known to the Celts is the Bean Si (banshee), which is Gaelic for a Faerie woman. In her book, *An Encyclopedia of Fairies*, folklorist, Katherine Briggs writes that "In the Highlands of Scotland she is also called, BEAN-NIGHE, or the LITTLE-WASHER-BY-THE-FORD, because she is seen by the side of a burn or river washing the blood-stained clothes of those about to die."[19]

The Banshee is known in Celtic folklore as a Faerie woman whose scream announces the impending death of a family member. The scream is called in Gaelic a *caoine*, which translates to 'keening or lamenting'. It was thought that each family had its own Banshee, which appeared in various forms from crone to beautiful young woman often wearing a veil or shroud.

In Scotland the brownie was common to the people of the Highlands, Lowlands and Islands, as well as the inhabitants of much of England. A brownie is usually a Faerie man, short in stature, about three-feet high, with a worn-looking face and shaggy head, clothed in brown rags. While the inhabitants of the house slept, the brownie busied himself with chores and by morning they were greeted by freshly brewed beer and churned butter. A brownie's chores also included tending to the farm animals and sweeping the floors. Care had to be taken with regard to gifts of appreciation as the brownie was easily offended and would leave permanently if insulted. Gifts of clothing were a great insult and the brownie would never be seen again.

Katherine Briggs also writes,

> ...the housewife was careful not to offer the tidbit to the brownie, only to leave it in its reach. Any offer of reward for its services drove the brownie away; it seemed to be an absolute TABOO. This was

accounted for in various ways. In Berwickshire it was said that the brownie was the appointed servant of mankind to ease the weight of Adam's curse and was bound to serve without payment; another suggestion was that he was of too free a spirit to accept the bondage of human clothes or wages; sometimes again that he was bound to serve until he was considered worthy of payment; or again, it might be the quality of the goods offered that offended him, as in the story of the Lincolnshire brownie, who, most unusually, was annually given a linen shirt, until a miserly farmer, succeeding to the farm, left him out one of coarse sacking, on which he sang:

> Harden, harden, harden hamp!
> I will neither grind nor stamp.
> Had you given me linen gear,
> I had served you many a year,
> Thrift may go, bad luck may stay,
> I shall travel far away.

With which he left the farm never to return.[20]

A *gruagach* was a wild, long-haired female spirit, native to the Scottish Highlands. Her home was in the pasture where she looked after the cows. Fresh milk was poured into hollow stones as a nightly offering and failure to do so could bring sickness or death to a cow the following morning. These stones are known today as basin stones or 'gruagach stones'. In her book, *Touchstones for Today*, Alanna Moore wrote, "In the Scottish highlands the Stone of the Long Haired One (Clach na Gruagach) at Gairloch had offerings of milk given to the Gruagach daily, in a tradition that continued right up to the early 20th century. Should the dairy maids neglect to do this, trouble would always follow!"[21]

Certain races of Faerie were to be avoided at all costs. In the Scottish Highlands the *Sluagh* are a dreaded Faerie race known as The Host of the Unforgiven Dead. The *Sluagh* have long been feared, as they come forth at night and spread misfortune and illness. They were said to have the power to create a searing wind that would burn the skin and cause painful boils, and they were known for fierce battles that took place in the sky, appearing like a black cloud of starlings, where their blood from battle would fall to the Earth. In *The Vanishing People*, Katharine Briggs writes, "The bright red lichen called *crotal* is supposed to be the blood of the *Sluagh*. But they are not content with fighting among themselves. They swoop down from the sky and snatch up mortal men and employ them to shoot darts at their fellow men, and at cattle and horses, dogs and cats."[22]

The Selkie is a Scottish Faerie creature. The large seals whose habitat is the waters around the Orkney Islands are called 'the Selkie folk' in old folklore. It is said they are a race of humans whose home is in the ocean where they clothe themselves in seal skins to "move from one region of air to another", according to Katherine Briggs. Seen without their skins, the Selkie men and women are more beautiful than ordinary people. Many a story has been told of naked and comely Selkie women seen sunning themselves on rocks next to their skins. It was not common for Selkie women to seek out mortal men as lovers but at times they were captured by men of the islands who stole their skins. The male Selkies however, were known to leave the ocean and claim earthly women as their lovers though they never stayed as lifelong partners. If a child was born from this coupling, they had webbed hands and feet, which if cut, produced horny growths making some tasks almost impossible.

There is a heart-wrenching ballad from Snarra Voe on the island of Shetland called 'The Grey Selkie of Sule Skerry', that was collected from a Shetland woman. Seven verses of it were published by Captain F.W.L. Thomas in the 1850's. The ballad tells of a human woman who laments that she doesn't know the father of her nursing babe. He comes to her in her bed and says,

> I am a man upo the lan,
> An I am a silkie in the sea;
> And when I'm far and far frae lan,
> My dwelling is in Sule Skerrie

He gives her a purse of gold in return for his Selkie son and prophesies that she will one day marry a gunner who will shoot both him and his son.[23]

I encourage you to listen to the hauntingly beautiful voice of Joan Baez singing part of this ballad, titled, 'Silkie'.[24]

Trees are sacred to the Faeries, particularly the Hawthorne. An old Irish saying goes, 'Woe betide he or she who dares to fell a Faerie tree'. As a result of that sentiment there are groves and Faerie forts in both Ireland and Scotland that remain intact today. The Faerie prefer the wild places where they will not be disturbed and the traditional people took great care to be respectful. A Faerie fort is a circular ancient archeological site consisting of earthen mounds or embankments. They are said to be home to the Faerie and portals to the otherworld, and even those who profess not to believe in such things will nonetheless refrain from disturbing an associated site for fear of potential repercussions.

Indeed, there are stories of foolish souls who used stones from a fairy fort to build their home and fell into misfortune as a result. Even if available, one would never take wood from a tree located within such a fort, nor would one ever disturb the fort to make way for farmland, etc. Farmers in the past would often leave a Faerie tree (often a Hawthorne) alone, plowing around it but never disturbing it regardless of whether they believed such things or not. There are too many stories told of farmers who disturbed a stone structure or Faerie grove and lost numbers of their herd to a mysterious illness. As well, there are Faerie paths and walkways that run in a straight line between traditional archeological sites like Faerie forts and raths, as well as rock monuments, springs, hills, etc. These pathways are used by the Faeries to get from site to site and local people through time knew full well of them. If someone was foolish enough to build a house or barn that obstructed a Faerie path the repercussions were most unpleasant. It was not uncommon for illness or even death to befall humans or animals as a result.

In *The Secret Country*, authors Janet and Colin Bord write,

A graphic demonstration of the inadvisability of obstructing a fairy path is given in the following story. The events related took place in the 1930's, and the author of *The Middle Kingdom* (where the details come from) did not identify people, or places because at the time of his writing the story 'is too poignant.' A family was experiencing a great deal of sorrow because, one after another, four children sickened and died, leaving doctors baffled. The fifth child became ill and was near death, and so the doctor was amazed when the child's father hurried to tell him that the boy was well again—and that there would be no more deaths. Apparently, the father had gone to a wise woman to see if she could throw any light on the tragedies, and she immediately saw what was wrong. A few months before the first illness, the father had built an extension to his house, but this was badly placed for it 'just obstruded into a straight line between two neighboring fairy forts.' The wise woman advised him to demolish the extension, which he did the same night, and then found the dying child was much improved. This tale also illustrates the importance attached to the correct siting of buildings[25]...

The Christianized beliefs tell of Faeries as being fallen angels and it is said that when Lucifer was expelled from heaven other angels fell with him. Some landed in water and became mermaids while others fell on land and became Faeries. In Scotland, Wales, England and Ireland, children were cautioned to keep away from Faerie mounds and certain trees that were thought to be portals into the Faerie realms. This was a common form of propaganda put forth by the Church. We know that early Christian monks put to paper many Celtic myths adding their own Christianized slant. We have them to thank for preserving the myth and story that would otherwise have been lost. That said, a number of years ago I read the heartbreaking story, *The Children of Lyr*, about the children beloved by their father, Lir, of the De Danann, and resented by his jealous new wife. She turned them into swans for three hundred years and the story tells of their difficulty through that time. I wept as I read the story only to get to the end where the children as swans, professed their faith in the 'true God' and were baptized. I recognized that the story had been Christianized and I was both angered and disappointed.

Such a beautiful, sad story and we'll never know the original ending. John Duncan, the Scottish symbolist artist, painted a gorgeous image of the children of Lyr in 1914.

The Children of Lir, John Duncan, 1924.
(Dundee Art Galleries and Museums collection.)

Mushrooms, Faeries and Seers

An observed phenomenon with mushrooms is their propensity to appear in a circle on grass or woodland, or around a tree, seemingly out of nowhere in mere hours. We now know that this is caused by the hyphae, (mycelial threads) beneath the ground. The hyphae secrete enzymes from their tips, taking in nutrients from the soil. This breaks down larger molecules that are then absorbed by the walls of the hyphae. The hyphae then grow outwardly in a circular fashion. Once the nutrients in the center have been fully consumed, that part dies off and forms a ring on the ground above. After a year, mushrooms sprout from the ground to form a circle. Over the years, the circle grows larger to where it can go from a foot or two in diameter to over thirty feet.

Even though the how of this natural occurrence is known and understood, it is no less magical when one happens upon such a circle. In the past, people thought these strange appearances were supernatural and they became known as 'Faerie rings'. These magical rings were associated with the spirit world, which inspired folklore that stirred the imaginations of many. The rings were said to be places of fertility and good fortune, heralding the arrival of spring, and it was thought that nearby crops and livestock would benefit. A common belief was that Faeries and other supernatural beings would dance around the rings in the dark of night. Poet, William Butler Yeats referred to this in his poetic play, *The Land of Heart's Desire*, writing,

> While the faeries dance in a place apart,
> Shaking their milk-white feet in a ring,
> Tossing their milk-white arms in the air...

It was also thought that a Faerie ring was a portal to the Otherworld. People were warned to avoid entering the circle for fear of being forced into unrelenting dance that could cause extreme exhaustion and even madness. Other names such as 'sorcerer's rings' and 'witches rings', became known, lending to the potential danger these rings could pose.

Circular structures found in the British Isles such as stone circles, ring forts and circular mounds have captivated the imagination and their connection to the Faerie races has always been known. An old poem from Britannia's Pastorals states:

> Near to this wood there lay a pleasant mead,
> Where fairies often did their measures tread,

Which in the meadows made such circles green,
As if with garlands it had crowned been...
Within one of these rounds was to be seen
A hillock rise, where oft the Fairy-Queen
At twilight sate.

The Fairy Ring, Walter Jenks Morgan (1847-1924).

The people of the Victorian era were enchanted by the Faerie, and artists of that time produced delightful images of little winged sprites, elves and Faeries. However, traditional Faerie do not present with wings and they possess a grander countenance than the fanciful images depicted by such artists. There are tiny flower Faeries who are connected to the tending of blossoms but this book is focusing on the larger races of Faerie. Interestingly though, the fanciful images of the winged Faerie often depicted them near or on toadstools or the red capped mushroom, *Amanita muscaria*. Though these were familiar images to the Victorians, there was no awareness in the general public of the psychedelic strains at that time, despite the fact that Liberty Cap (*Psilocybe semilanceata*), and Wavy Cap (*Psilocybe cyanescens*), among others grow wild all over the British Isles.

Amanita muscaria differs from the psilocybe mushroom. It contains very different chemical constituents and it produces its own kind of visionary trance state. It may very well have been used by the Druids for initiation and ritual purposes, as it grows all over the British Isles and is very distinctive, and would definitely not have escaped the eyes of the natives. There are stories in the old Irish tales of magical apples, the ingestion of which transported the character to the Otherworld. Could that be in truth the Amanita mushroom that would be found growing around the base of trees? Peter Lamborn Wilson wrote an entire book on the subject, titled, *Ploughing the Clouds: The Search for Irish Soma*.

One such story that features an enchanted apple tells of Connla of the fiery hair who is the son of the king, Conn of the Hundred Fights. On a walk with his father, Connla encountered a beautiful Faerie maiden that only he could see though his father was able to hear her. She invited Connla to come with her to the Otherworld to live forever, expressing her love for him. His father called his druid to send her away and before she disappeared, she tossed Connla an apple and for an entire month he would eat nothing else, for every night the apple replenished itself. During that time Connla yearned to be with her again.

At the end of a month Connla stood on the Plain of Arcomin with his father when the Faerie maiden again appeared to him. Once again, she invited him to join her in the land of Tir Na N'og, where Connla would be king and live forever. Torn between his love for the Faerie maiden and his love for his people, he chose the Faerie maiden and boarded her crystal boat, sailing away to the Otherworld, never to be seen again.

Is this one of a number of veiled metaphors told as mythical story for the power of the Amanita muscaria to transform the initiate in a way that changes him forevermore? We will likely never know, as the rituals of the Druids were secret and nothing was written down. That said, the Druids were known for their magical practices and extensive knowledge of both the medicinal and magical properties of plants. Personally, I don't doubt that the ancient people of the British Isles utilized the visionary fungi of both psilocybin mushrooms and Amanita muscaria for their rites and rituals. Take that with a grain of salt if you will, and consider reading Peter Lamborn Wilson's illuminating book.

In *The Fairy Mythology*, Keightley speaks of mushrooms and elves along with the Shakespearean character, Puck, writing,

> A further proof perhaps of Puck's rural and extern character is the following rather trifling circumstance. An old name of the fungus named puff ball is puckfist, which is plainly, Puck's fist, and not puff-fist as Nares conjectured; for its Irish name is Cos-a-Phooka or Pooka's foot, i.e., Puck's-foot. We will add, by the way, that the Anglo Saxon Wolfs-fist, is rendered in the dictionaries toadstool, mushroom, and we cannot help suspecting that as wolf and elf were sometimes confounded, and wolf and fist are in fact incompatible terms, this was originally Elfs-fist, and that the mushrooms meant were not the thick ugly toadstools, the 'grislie toadstools' of Spencer, but those delicate fungi called in Ireland, fairy mushrooms, and which perhaps in England were also ascribed to the fairies.[26]

In his book, Peter Lamborn Wilson points out that the Liberty Cap mushroom with its distinctive wispy stems is a dead ringer for Keightley's description, "those delicate fungi called in Ireland, fairy mushrooms." I do not think it's a stretch to say that there were a few intrepid souls in days of old who knew full well the end results of eating such a mushroom. The fact that it was associated with Faeries is a glaringly obvious detail. The Irish name, Cos-a-Phooka or Pooka's foot refers to a type of shape-shifting Faerie found near mounds and ancient stones. Wilson writes, "...the Pooka seems to have been a more formidable character, and a shape-shifter, able to assume many forms, and to cause humans to assume fairy reality in the form of visions, transformations and hallucinations...In colloquial modern Irish the Liberty Cap is called a "pookie" or little Pooka."[27]

In his article titled, "The Mead of Inspiration", ethnopharmacologist,

Christian Ratsch, Ph.D., speaks to the use of psychedelic substances in mead and beer. He writes,

> In the history of brewing there are probably no plants we currently recognize as psychoactive that *haven't* been added to beer at some particular time or place. The ancient Egyptians brewed a mandrake beer; the Indians spiked their corn beer (*chicha*) with coca leaves, datura seeds, and morning glory seeds; in the Orient beer was improved with hashish and opium, and in Siberia dried fly agaric mushrooms (*Amanita muscaria*) were crumbled into the beer. The ancient Gauls brewed beer from darnel, and in the Middle Ages, thin beers were spiced with cinnamon, nutmeg and cardamon. The addition of hops to beer is an invention of Christian monks. The brethren of the monastery were not to be stimulated by beer additives with aphrodisiac effects; to the contrary, they should be sedated by the hops. The heathen mead of inspiration was no simple beer or simple mead, but must have been a psychoactive drink whose intoxicating components would have had a stimulating effect on creativity. We know of various Indo-European traditions in which plant preparations served as sources of inspiration for the singers and poets: the Soma of the Aryans, the *bhang* of the Brahmins, the mushroom wine of Dionysus.[28]

Many today who've ingested psychoactive fungi and plants have experienced visions of Elves, Faeries and other nature spirits, as well as deities, departed relatives and friends, and some have conversed with trees, plants and animals while so imbued. As well, there have always been certain people throughout time who've possessed natural psychic abilities. Those who can see the otherwise unseen have what the Irish call 'the second sight', and they perceive and communicate with invisible intelligences without the need of any psychoactive substance. They are especially sensitive, with a natural inborn ability to communicate with the spirit world. In *The Secret Commonwealth of Elves, Fauns and Fairies*, written in the 17th century, Reverend R. Kirk spoke of "men of the second sight," adding, "females being seldom so qualified," and told numerous stories of their accurate portendings and sightings of the Faerie.

Those with the second sight often served their communities utilizing their gifts of heightened perception, clairvoyance and innate knowing to act as wise man or woman, psychic, magician, poet or healer.

Today there continue to be individuals who possess 'the second sight', known by the Celts as *da sheallach,* which means to have two sights.

In the 17th century, Martin Martin wrote of the *da sheallach,* stating, "The second-sight is a singular faculty of seeing an otherwise invisible object without any previous means used by the person that sees it for that end; the vision makes such a lively impression upon the seers, that they neither see nor think of anything else except the vision as long as it continues...the seer knows neither the object, time nor place of a vision before it appears; and the same object is often seen by different persons, living at considerable distance from one another."[29]

Throughout the centuries, those who possessed the second sight apprenticed under the tutelage of a highly skilled teacher in the arts of seership and prophecy. After years of training, they could mediate for those on both sides of the veil. In her book, *Celtic Visions: Seership, Omens and Dreams of the Otherworld,* Caitlin Matthews writes, "For the people of the ancient Celtic world, seership opened windows into the otherworld. It awakened the essence of true vision and wisdom, which was known by the poets as the gléfiosa or 'the bright knowledge.' Seership is a means of understanding the connections between the two sides of reality; both the physical, manifest world that is perceptible by our everyday senses, as well as the invisible, unmanifest world that we perceive with our inner senses."[30]

For regular folk who do not possess the second sight, the mushroom is a natural portal into the unseen side of reality. Used with intention, it can catalyze spiritual growth and understanding by lifting the seeker beyond his limited place of awareness to a far greater place of knowing. As awareness is expanded in these states, one becomes acutely attuned to the surrounding environment, so that subtle energies that otherwise go undetected are now palpable. One discovers through direct experience the indwelling spirits of the natural world that our animist ancestors spoke of. Everything in Nature contains an animating force that is an intelligence that can be engaged.

A mushroom journey taken in a safe place outdoors can be incredibly profound. When I hosted retreats at my cottage in Vermont, there were a number of people who spent time outside during their mushroom journey and they were forever changed as a result. It was quite a thing to witness. One woman in particular who had suffered greatly over her life and had no interest in anything Faerie encountered a 'lady of the woods' who she said was shimmering and spectacularly beautiful. My client was in a state of awe and spent more than two hours in that place receiving messages from her and the surrounding trees. It is something she will never forget. Another time I watched a man who wished to sit at the picnic table for his journey and I could see he was utterly captivated. He sat there for almost the entire afternoon and when he came inside, he was a different person, gentled and humbled. Again, a very special thing to witness.

Our innate connection to the unseen intelligences of Nature has been severely compromised through the onslaught of the Industrial Revolution and the ensuing materialist ideologies that have been imposed upon the human consciousness like a plague, such as Prussian schooling, Marxism, Taylorism, the Theory of Relativity, consumerism, and others not worth mentioning. A sideways glance at the brutal, ugly cityscapes resulting from these ideologies fills one with grief for the heartless desacralization of the natural world.

On this subject author John Michell wrote, "The tall chimneys of industrialized landscape symbolize the excessive dominance of the masculine yang force and its values. The spirits of Nature are expelled from their haunts in tree, hill and stream, and the country is left sterile and dead, a monument to the consequences of human rapacity unchecked by consideration of spirit."[31]

We are now firmly ensconced in the Technological Revolution, which is making the Industrial Revolution look like child's-play in comparison. Our brains have changed not necessarily for the better with the incessant use of cellphones that put us in a mild trance and track our every move and utterance. Genes are being spliced and diced in animals, plants and humans. The wonders of A.I. have turned dark as we find ourselves surveilled both outside and inside our homes, and it is all too clear that this technology is being used to march us into a totalitarian dystopia.

The Celtic Revival began in the late 19th century and continued into the early 20th century throughout Ireland and the British Isles. It was a response to the rapacious intrusion and so-called, 'modernization' in the name of 'progress' of the Industrial Revolution, the effects of which were a scourge on the beauty of the land, seducing the mindset of the people and calling them away from their once treasured traditions and regard for Nature. The artisans, writers and poets of that time endeavored to invoke the folk soul, the spirituality and the beauty of the past in an effort to maintain a sense of the sacred. To see where we are now in terms of the disconnect from Nature and our own human Nature is truly disturbing and concerning.

Maybe, just maybe, we will experience a similar revival now in an effort to anchor some modicum of respect and honor for Nature and the sacred, and ultimately the sanctity of mankind. There are certainly growing numbers of people today who are embracing the land, homesteading, growing food and raising animals honorably using traditions of old. More people are exploring their ancestral roots and learning traditional skills in artisanship and traditional medicine practices. And many are seeking spiritually in an earnest desire to connect to the sacred, and bring that into a world of people who are lost in the machine.

In each and every one of us there lives a small, flickering flame of knowing. If we but open our hearts to the possibility that there is indeed an unseen world of intelligences to be discovered and engaged, we have a chance then of greeting that reality in our lifetime and infusing our world with its sacred magic, which will hopefully bring the unaware to their senses. Truth is stranger than fiction and nothing is as it seems. This Earth, a living entity, holds far more mystery and magic than we've been taught to believe, and the key to unlock that with all its gifts is held by the invisible spirits of Nature who watch and wait.

Fairy Folk Tree, Arthur Rackham, 1914. (In Imagina, by Julia Ellsworth Ford.)

Messages from the Forest Folk

The token of the word unheard, unspoken
Till the wind shake a thousand whispers from the yew.

– T. S. Eliot, Ash Wednesday, 1930, IV

Having taken my first half dozen mushroom journeys in the lush mossy splendor of the Washington rainforest, I developed there a subtle connection to the spirits of the forest, and that continued on my morning runs in the forest by my home in Redmond, Washington. Running affects brain activity and can take one into a mild waking dream state. It was during these runs that I would fall into a similar soft connection with the natural world around me, as if I'd ingested a tiny amount of mushrooms.

Under the influence of psychoactive mushrooms, one's senses are heightened, and I have clear memories of quiet communion with a small huckleberry bush that I laid next to within the grove of cedars where I would journey. Back home in Redmond while on my morning runs, I would see those same bushes among the trees and shrubbery and each time it would feel like I was seeing an old friend. Something very different was happening in me while on those trail runs that had nothing to do with the intellect. It was a sensorial and telepathic awareness of the many subtle vibrations all around me and each had its own frequency signature.

On one such run I received a poem that flowed in out of nowhere and I spent the rest of the run trying to remember the first couple of stanzas. As soon as I got home, I wrote them out and the rest of the poem poured forth like taking dictation. After that I began bringing my digital recorder with me on my runs just in case. Most of the time I was bathed in the quiet beauty of the woods, but a few times a poem came in as if an inner door had swung open, and in flowed the prose until the door closed as suddenly as it had opened.

There are many stories of people who have received stirring messages or poems while immersed in the natural world. One I read of recently was from Seán Pádraig O'Donoghue, who wrote in his Substack about a poem that came to him in its entirety. He stated, "This poem arose spontaneously in its complete form as I walked the road to Dún Aonghasa in June of 2018. The words of the ferryman are an almost exact transcription." Well, Dún Aonghasa is an Iron Age 'fort' on Inis Mór and these ancient places are said to be home to the Sidhe. In my chapter titled Scotland Magic, I explore the charge field of stones and our own biological charge field and how that makes us receptive to the wide variety of natural radiation fields found around the planet, particularly at megalithic sites. And Seán, himself, is particularly sensitive as a practicing medicine man/herbalist, teacher and poet. The entirety of the poem that came to him can be read in his gorgeous book, *Courting the Wild Queen,* and I will give you just the first two verses of this beautiful transmission below.

The dolphin rises,
guiding the ferry
toward Inis Mór
pulling into the quay,
the captain leans in
and tells you

history on this island
has layers

the waterman has
always had a connection
with the underworld

perhaps at
Dún Aonghasa
you will begin
to understand.

ii.

The road to
Dún Aonghasa
begins at Kilronan—

"Church of the Seal"
The god of love
insists you approach
not on your knees
but your feet,
their soles kissing
the body
of his Beloved[32]...

Dún Aonghasa, Inishmore, Aran Islands, Ireland.

The mind is a portal and we have far more ability to connect with the world of spirit than we even realize. My late teacher, Dr. Brugh Joy, MD, used to say that we are multi-dimensional beings. While psychoactive plants and fungi can deliver inspired mind-states, so too can quiet time in Nature, albeit in a more subtle way. That said, let us not dismiss the power of the subtle. It is through shifting our mind state that the still small voice, or what I call, words without sound, can reach us. For this, it is necessary to disconnect from the cacophony of discordance our modern construct has created, and still ourselves, preferably near or in a natural setting where the gift of inspiration can effectively reach us.

In this first series of transmissions, the majority of the poems came through on those morning forest runs. The last few transmissions, *Message from the Old Gods I-IV*, and *A Head's Up from the Trees*, came through while in a *be-mushroomed* state. The set of four *Messages from the Old Gods* entered while I was lying next to an Irish friend in a cabin in the Washington Rainforest. We were in silent darkness, journeying in the cloak of night in the Otherworld when I telepathically heard a number of women's voices around me singing in a language I didn't recognize till it occurred to me they were singing in Gaelic. Then men's voices joined in and I was transported by the haunting beauty of their song. After a few minutes, poetry began to come through and by then I knew to always have my digital recorder nearby when journeying, and I whispered the messages in as they came.

It was a few months later that I found myself on the Isle of Lewis in the Outer Hebrides of Scotland with Freddy Silva and an exceptional group of five intrepid souls. We were sitting together at the breakfast table before leaving to explore the stone circles when one of the participants asked me what I did. I mentioned my work with the mushroom then added that I bring through poetry and she asked if I would read one of the messages. I opened my phone and found the first *Message from the Old Gods*, and read it to the group. When I was finished you could have heard a pin drop. In that moment I clearly felt the magic of the poetry and its effects on those who listen. We were in a very special part of the world where the realm of Faerie is very much accessible. It was at the stone circle of Callanish where I stood alone and read aloud *Message from the Old Gods III*, under a heavy grey sky. I read it like a warrior declaring to the enemy their coming defeat and when I was finished, by God, the heavy grey clouds broke apart and bright sunlight streamed through. You couldn't have choreographed it more perfectly. My experiences in Scotland were out of the ordinary and profoundly transformative. The spirit of that land is still vibrant even today, and its stirring beauty is captivating and deeply inspiring.

The final poetic message in this series, *A Head's Up from the Trees*, also came through via the mushroom portal. I was in the Ho rainforest in Washington State hosting two women who had come for a retreat with me. They were inside the cabin on two sofas situated in front of a large picture window and they were deep in the realms. It was raining lightly outside and I stepped out to stand by the edge of the yard where down below, the Ho River flowed vigorously. I looked up at a large cedar tree before me and in came its sobering message. It has long been understood by cultures around the world that trees are a dwelling place for spirits, the dryads of Greece being a well-known example. John Michell writes,

> ...throughout the greater part of history, trees were considered the most respectable and enlightening companions, and it was the custom to ask their advice on the highest matters of state. They directed the wanderings of the earliest tribes, nor did civilization remove their influence. The Greeks consulted Apollo's laurel at Delphi and the oak of Zeus at Dodona, the Druid priests were intimate with the oracular oak, and the warning voice of the grove of Vesta saved Rome from attack by the Gauls. The Church and human pride destroyed the old relationship between men and trees, and so Joan of Arc, inspired by a tree spirit, was burnt for observing the orthodox prophetic tradition.[33]

Well, I talk to trees and they talk back to me. And I know there are many people who would say the same. In spite of how unconscious the majority of the population is at this time there seems to be a persistent undercurrent of nature-spirit energy that reaches a certain number of folks who are touched by and feel a kinship with the spirits of these extraordinary wonders of Nature. I felt that *A Head's Up from the Trees* was a perfect finish to this series of forest messages and one that puts a punctuation mark on the ancient wisdom Nature holds if we would just pause and listen.

Call of the Wee Folk

Woman who runs fast through our woods
Whose lungs breathe deep the morning air
Your heart beats strong beneath your breast
The sun lights up your long blonde hair

It pleases us to see how much you cherish Nature's beauty
We feel in you a call to arms, a sense of moral duty
We know of those who come to you to grow and heal their pain
We tell you now (because you doubt), your work is not in vain

The time has come upon the Earth, the hour is at hand
You all must wake and see the mess within and on your land
We hold the healing medicines, the soothing balms for all your kin
We say you must continue to assist Earth's children to begin
A new embrace of how to live upon their goddess, Terra
That shuns the curse of greed and hate that threatens this new era

To those who endeavor to serve the Earth in a myriad of different ways
We encourage you to stay the course despite the collective haze
Of apathy and ignorance and addiction to diversions
We say to all, you must prevail in spite of the perversions
Spend some time in Nature's embrace and let us into your mind
We've guidance and many wonders to share with you and all your kind
Encourage the spellbound to partake of Nature's bounty and healing
Gently urge them away from their toys and into the depths of feeling
The suffering of many can be replaced with knowledge of purpose that's pure
Those who've lost their way in life can rebirth to a path that is sure
For all are called now to the gate
Your actions will decide your fate

And so dear woman who loves the trees
Who whispers to moss and cares for the bees
Do know that we are watching you and all your kind whose hearts are true
We do not push, we wait for you to make the effort to construe
Our words of guidance and urgency
Hoping that you all will see
How cherished you are on this blessed Earth
How essential your actions as you birth
An era of awakening
Of consciousness, of hearts that sing
A song of life, not death and destruction
A song that offers wise instruction
Of how to live on Mother Terra
That insures the dictates of this new era
Will cede to the council of Elfin and Fae
Whose knowledge of the green arts may
Turn back the direction of damage done
Calling back a sense of fun
Of reverence and loving care for all
Respond dear humans to our call...

Forest Folk

Down a path of mossy green
I'm led to magic sight unseen
The trees instruct me,
"Take this turn, sit by the stream and you will learn."

Breathless, I take in the sight
A brook flows briskly to the right
Its water, crystal clear and cold
I dip my hands and then I'm told

"Dear one, you must still your mind
And tune in to a different kind
Of folk who live among the moss
Look for a bridge that you can cross.

It can't be seen by human eyes
But if you're still you'll realize
The bridge exists within your mind
The wee folk call you to their kind..."

I closed my eyes and stilled my thoughts
And listened to the reverie
Of water babbling quickly by
And dancing over rockery

And then I felt a strange sensation
Something soft caressed my cheek
A subtle whisper in my ear said,
"Dear one, we know what you seek."

"We are the magic forest folk
And dear, we know how much you care
When you bow to moss and tree
We hear your thoughts within the air.
We tell you now this world is changing

What will happen? Who can say?
But know that we're in this together
Know that there will come a day.

We herald a grand reckoning
When man will see his great mistake
We know you wish this day to come
And fear that it will come too late.

Yet we say when hearts are pure
When will is strong, intention sure
A realization can arise
That for some time has been disguised.

A potent spell was cast on you
And when it breaks among the few
You'll realize unbridled power
That summons wisdom to the hour.

Great minds and hearts will gather insight
Groups will form to lead and highlight
Action that will bring a change.
And though some will think it strange
They'll come around, they'll have no choice
And through good leaders we will voice
Our good guidance for correction
To initiate the resurrection
Of mankind's bond with all of Nature...

We will work with you, dear one
And all your folk who humbly come
The invisible bridge that can't be seen
Will appear where it has always been.
Mankind will then have eyes to see
And ears to hear the reverie
And Nature will lead once again
All her children finally sane..."

Pact with the Fae

You wish a rhyme from Fae to thee?
Well, we'll provide you one that's free
You pledged today to serve our kin
To still your mind and go within
To listen closely to the sound
That hails from folk close to the ground
We led you to the moss-clad tree
Where you found the temple door
In your dream state you'll return
And shrink in size to forest floor

An emissary will be waiting
You must look him in the eye
Offer him the finest honey
Say to him, "The time is nigh
For Faeries, Elves, and all to dance
Under the Moon in a magic trance."

And among the ferns and mossy rocks
Will appear the Fae in luminous frocks
Their elfin cousins will nod their heads
And gather the glistening fragile threads
Of spider webs woven from branch to twig
The Elfin do not care a fig
If spider's disturbed or even its prey
For a new web is born at the break of day

These threads are used to weave a pathway
Deep beneath the roots of the tree
Follow the Faerie cavalcade
To a shimmering place few humans see
This is a place of secret knowledge
Think of it as a Faerie college
Where ancient secrets are held with care
And the green arts are practiced everywhere

In small doses we'll reveal to you
The magical practices known to few
Commit yourself to this ancient craft
As we present you with each draft
Of precious knowledge and magical working
And once we begin there can be no shirking
Of what is expected when you enlist
The help of beings few know exist

Communion with Faeries from times long past
Was known to your ancestors who held fast
To the sacred and secret knowledge of old
That was held by the Fae whose stories were told
By those who've engaged them and treated them well
And returned with extraordinary stories to tell
Some of our kin are dangerous sorts
Who cause many problems and harm
Yet others of us will form solid bonds so do not feel alarm

We only require you open your heart and speak from a place that is true
We always check for integrity before we reveal a clue
For magic and knowledge is best held by those who keep their ears close to the ground
Who see with real eyes and know when to speak and when to not make a sound

And so dear woman who seeks what is hidden and held behind the veil
We'll assist your noble endeavor to drink from the Holy Grail
Use your time wisely and don't waste a chance to still and listen well
To the beings of Nature and worlds beyond
Gently coax them from their shell

Their language is filled with symbol and riddle and rhymes of every kind
Open the door within your soul and hear them in your mind
They'll initiate you in myriad ways
They'll enter your dreams and transform your days
So welcome to Wyrd, dear woman of heart
Your pledge was heard
Where shall we start?

Pledge to the Bee

Thy majesty, our dear queen bee
Thy fate seems sealed if man can't see
The commercialization of Nature's garden
Has caused the hearts of man to harden

The hubris of man as he splices genes
The spraying of poisons on fields of green
The skies crisscrossed with chemical spray
I fear that there will come a day

When the blossom of fruit tree and scented flower
Lies sterile without the bee's sweet power
To suckle the nectar with loving care
In a sensual dance that brings to bear
All manner of bounty, a radiant feast
That feeds and delights both man and beast

Thy majesty and maintainer of beauty
I pledge to thee my solemn duty
To care for the land with a sensitive touch
Guided by Nature that teaches me such

That celestial and telluric forces
Respond to certain specific courses
Of actions that don't follow popular science
But follow a higher cosmic alliance

Oh, dear bees, I shall not rest
As long as my heart beats beneath my breast
I'll write, I'll speak, I'll share the magic
Of remedies to prevent the tragic
Loss of you and so many creatures
Whose presence in my garden features
Largely as I hear the song
Of bee and bird—oh, how I long

To see the hearts of mankind awaken
And return to Nature what has been taken
By working with Earth instead of against her
We call back the beauty and cast out the gangster
Whose plunder has caused such harm and disgrace
To the character of the human race

This is our time to save not just the bee
But all creatures and humanity
Our moment is now, the time is here
Take action, all, and do not fear
For the spirit of man and woman is true
And the Goddess is calling me and you

To summon our authority
And gather our community
To begin to act with sanity
As we recreate with dignity

A planet of people who act with grace
And restore consciousness to the human race
I hold this vision as what can be
When people remember their sovereignty

Oh blessed pollinators, dear
Your warnings we hear loud and clear
I know that we have the power to heal
And hold to ourselves a new ideal

This is my vision-quest in life
May the bees prevail as we end this strife...

The Oracle

The seers of old knew our kind well
As dust-covered books will surely tell
They journeyed to worlds not known by their folk
They put forth their offerings and with courage spoke

With respectful intention to gently commune
To taste of the magic that comes when the Moon
Shines brightly, its luminous light on the glen
Where the mushroom caps gleam in the brightness and then
She picks just the ones that whisper and call
And ritually eats them, stems and all

And behold it appears, the door to the sages
Who've spoken through oracles down through the ages
The seer approaches with heart open wide
Light as a feather with nothing to hide

She bares her soul bravely and ventures to ask
If entry is possible so she can bask
In the secret and mystical ethers of knowledge
Where keepers of wisdom hold court in a college
Known only to those whose hearts betray
Their burning desire to learn the ways

Of legendary mythical beings of story
Whose noble exploits brought power and glory
To people who've long left this planet behind
Yet still, there are those who wish to find
The beauty that once was known to so many
The oracle asks if it's possible any
Good spirit can make itself known to her now...

And lo comes the owl in soft, silent flight
Its great wings shimmering in the moonlight
Then standing before the oracle's eyes
Is a lady in white who doesn't disguise
Her love and affection for this good priestess
Whose training spans lifetimes that highlight her prowess

As alchemist, herbalist, woman who heals
As prophetess, seer, and woman who kneels
On the sacred ground where the roots of the tree
Plumb deeply beneath her and lead her to see

The ancestral inhabitants living below
Who take her hand, and help her to know
The source of her own roots held by the earth
That shows her the memories she had before birth...

Come Fly with Us

This mystery lies hidden in view
Yet sadly is known to only a few
With eyes and ears that can perceive
And the imagination to conceive

Of worlds within worlds where beings of knowledge
Hold secrets contained in an ancient college
That all can access who have the heart
And burning desire to learn the art

Of speaking a language of foreign tongue
Learned through a medium growing in dung
An unlikely place for a ship to be found
That transports the seeker from common ground
To spectacular wonders that fly in the face
Of reason and rule that restricts your race
To a prison of mind that holds you back
And colors your imagination black

Come fly with us and you will discover
A wondrous place that is like no other
A place of connection to all that is dear
A place long known to the ancient seer
Who humbly travelled with open heart
Whose intention was pure from the very start

This place has cures for what ails your folk
And wisdom that feeds the fires you stoke
The beings who dwell in these places are real
Known only to those who are able to feel

We watch you all from behind the veil
We possess what you call the Holy Grail
It can only be accessed by breaking the spell
It is then you can drink from the sacred well
Of knowledge and truth and noble intentions
That transcend the constructs of man's inventions

Come fly with us, dear seekers who yearn
Whose souls ache for truth, whose beating hearts burn
For communion with shimmering beings of light
We offer you the gift of sight

We offer it freely in spite of your rules
Made by those who play you for fools
Our worlds offer freedom to be and express
To call forth your Nature that is no less
Than magnificent in its radiance and beauty
Wake now dear humans
That is your duty...

Keepers of the Beauty Way

Long this Earth has watched the many
O'er time their journeys laid
Multitudes of actors playing
Stories of the times they strayed

Far from home
That place of knowing
To a different garden
Where they'd be sowing
Seeds that offer them a chance
To engage in a wondrous earthly dance

Now some sojourners kept their sense of kinship with the mystery
Seeing past the passion play and accessing an earthly key
That took them deep beneath the surface story of the day
Into direct connection with the keepers of the beauty way

This key grows wild and close to the ground
It calls to the seer without a sound
It beckons with silent extended hand
And bonds the seer to a luminous band
Of shimmering light-filled beings who hold
The ancient secrets and magic of old

This key confers wisdom to those who come
With humble heart, retreating from
The madness of crowds and the cult of delusion
The seer is seeking an ancient solution

That takes her into the realms of truth
And bequeaths her with the ripened fruit
Of knowledge, wisdom, and understanding
She receives it all without commanding
Then gratefully thanks the beings of light
And makes her way home in the dark of the night

And by day she acts in service to all
Earth's beings whose suffering begs her call
She administers herbs with expert care
She burns magical plants that clear the air

Then she speaks with wisdom and clarity
Conferring light so they can see
And experience epiphany
And for those with curiosity
Who desire to learn the mystery
Whose hearts are pure and ready for knowledge
She'll guide them to that secret college

Found near the trees, those sages of old
This college springs forth from the ground in a bold
Explosion of unbridled reverie
Playful and teasing with unabashed glee

To greet yet another seeker who yearns
To taste of the deeper knowing that burns
In their heart, where the memory of where they came from
Calls them to Nature to apprentice with some
Of the greatest teachers the Earth has known
Whose wisdom and kindness has expertly sown

Threads that connect the mind with the heart
Threads that ensure Earth's people will start
To live once again with extended hand
Held fast to Nature and that shimmering band
Of magical beings whose colleges grow
Up from the fertile ground below...

A New Mindset

The spells that bind the untrained mind
And steer it away from truth
Must be sought out with keen intrepid care
And the expertise of a sleuth

For the crafty lies of the potentates
Who divide the masses and stir up hate
Must be brought to the light of awareness now
As the Earth seeks to show her children how

To access wisdom, knowledge, and truth
In hopes that it reaches the burgeoning youth
Who will carry the torch passed from elders, wise
For now it is time to realize

That the long-held secrets kept shadowed are found
From plants and fungi that grow in the ground
Beneath your very feet that walk
It is with you they wish to talk

These are ancient teachers and sages of old
Who instructed initiates who once were told
To carefully tend to the sacred wisdom
To pass it forward from kingdom to kingdom

And now as this precious Earth cries out
The initiates of old are instructed to shout
To the sleeping masses who are losing ground
To wake up now so they can found
A pathway home to truth and light
And wisdom that cuts through the dark of this night

The plant teachers break the sorcerer's spell
The fungi will lead you from possible hell
To clarity where creativity flows
Where the mind now free, is able to sow
The solutions so needed to heal this great Earth
To bring us together as kindreds to birth
A new manner of living together on Terra
That brings peace to the forefront of this new era

That casts out the trickery, deceit, and lies
And brings you to where you can realize
Yourselves as noble sons and daughters
Flowing within the earthly waters
Of beauty and wisdom and kindly intention
That fans the flames of a new invention

Birthed from opening the gates of the heart
Earth's offerings will guide you where to start
To heal and repair the damage done
To all Earth's beings under the Sun

The mushroom spirits have much to teach
Though some naysayers will call that a reach
Yet the keepers of wisdom are rising today
And they're just getting started in having their say

So be glad in your hearts, dear ones who fret
We will see that Earth's people do not forget
Their intrinsic magic and depth of soul
Earth's mystical offerings will make them whole...

Whispers from the Old Gods I

Coming changes to your plane
Coming changes once again
Rest your head dear earthly friend
Rest your heart so we can send
Messages from those afar
Coming to you in this hour

Songs are sung of once again
Meeting on this earthly plane
The gods of old returning now
They'll have your back
So you'll know how
To open all the doors now locked
You hold the key it is not blocked

We surround you and your friend
We are here until the end
We hold you in ancestral love
An ancient symbol is the dove
That flies from here to yonder there
To ensure that you're aware

Of we, the watchers of your kind
An ancient spell you will unbind
Within the power of your mind
Soon you will not be so blind...

Whispers from the Old Gods II

Speaking in a reverie
Poetic speech will come to thee
Words alight upon your tongue
Called forth from a college found in dung

Clever you, you ancient bard
Though you feel you've just a shard
Of what you had so long ago
We promise that quite soon you'll know

Access to a treasure trove
Of poetry and mythos old
Those who've loved you come again
And greet you on this earthly plane

Friends so dear you've never known
We'll light the way, for you it's shown
That you a keeper of wisdom be
Brought here so others on Earth can see

Stir their hearts, dear daughter of light
Illuminate the dark of night
Sing your song of sweetness bright
Prepare yourself for worthy fight
An ancient one of dark and light
Your moment's now, do not feel fright
For we surround you all through time
As we supply you with this rhyme

We send you grace and every kindness
We remove your earthly blindness
Here's the map so you can find us
Reunited once again

All the trees and faerie folk
Come to you as you invoke
Your light of heart, integrity
One and all, we come to see
This beauty being once again
Walking on the earthly plane...

Whispers from the Old Gods III

Trying to kill the gods of old?
How many times have you been told
We live as a spark or a blazing flame
When our people suffer we know who to blame
You may think you've got this one in the bag
We will see who flies the winner's flag

The trail of blood and suffering
Of travesties and broken wings
Yet we'll prevail, we are the light
You can't put out our candle bright

You suck the land of all its life
You plunder, kill, and create strife
And yet we live, we breathe, we fly
And we see through your lying eyes

Your day will come when you will die
The dark-winged ones will no more fly
Relief and rescue of our kin
This ancient battle we will win

When in time, you wish to know?
The wind will tell you when it blows
To set the course to sail our ship
The tables we will surely flip...

Whispers from the Old Gods IV

You sit in quiet candlelight
As guardian to friend in flight
Your dedication to your art
Has brought us here to help you start
The dawning of a new mindset
We're here to help you, though you fret

Dear earthly warrior priestess queen
We're here to say that you've been seen
You have our ear and we have yours
Our ships have landed on your shores

The treasures we have brought are many
Ask us and we'll give you any
Wand you wish to cast your spell
To call your people from their hell

A daunting task, dear, yes, we know
Yet we are here to help you throw
A lifeline cast out to the sea
For the drowning ones whose plea
For help to guide them through the gale
Will be answered, and their sail
Will steer their ship to calmer shores
Where they can access all the stores

Of ancient knowledge left behind
When mankind fell and became blind...

A 'Heads-Up' from the Trees

We shower you with hues of green
We create a stirring scene
We stand here and watch you all
And as the season moves to fall
We ready now for winter's sleep
When our roots that plumb Earth, deep

Absorb telluric frequencies
So we can gather energy
And cycle into spring anew
Resplendent in the morning dew

Elements of living sculpture
We inspire many cultures
We stand tall as the World Tree
In us lives the mystery

Come to us and we will teach you
People, hear us, we beseech you
Do not take our folk for granted
Just because we're easily planted
Doesn't mean we'll quickly grow
And to you our fruit bestow

You are told, "respect your elders"
This is also true of alders
And the oak and evergreens
The great old trees that once were seen
And beheld with humbled awe
Vast sculptures that were without flaw
Then sadly felled with axe and saw

You think we'll be here for always
Ever treated to displays

Of fruits and greens for all of you
But we will say that's just not true
The casual attitudes of today
Take us for granted, we're afraid

How easily we are cut down
The tragic sight when we hit ground
Displaced are many creatures, small
Who look for shelter in our tall
Inviting trunks and branches, strong
They know it's here that they belong

The forest is a library
It's home to many you can't see
A delicate menagerie
Of living beings magically
Connected to a wondrous web
Spanning Earth so all are fed

These forests found from north to south
Providing food for many mouths
Are canopies that must be held
With greatest care, not greedily felled

Take time away from all the toys
Spend time with we who're being destroyed
By the gloating corporate fools
Who look to us as simply tools
And miss the mark entirely
Their metal monsters storm our trees
And scar the land deplorably
And proudly plant their franken-seeds

This steep fall in the mind of man
Must be fixed if it possibly can
For this charade cannot last long

As steadily the birds whose song
Imparts a sound field for the Earth
Begins to fade till there's a dearth

Of birds and insects and much more
Till only silence greets your door
And that is when good hearts will break
Man's coarse inventions you'll forsake...

Callanish, Sir Henry James, 1866.

Scotland Magic

*The bard, prophet and mystic frequent the wild places of the earth,
where the disturbed energies of the earth spirit disorder the mind and
stimulate the poetic imagination.*

   – John Michell, *The Earth Spirit: It's Ways, Shrines and Mysteries*

Some things in life are fated and feel almost scripted. A year or so before going to Scotland I was in the Yucatan co-leading a small tour with my shaman teacher, Miguel Angel. We took the group to Palenque for the day where they would have the opportunity to explore the site and soak up its beauty. By then I had experienced a number of mushroom journeys where I had engaged with spirits, so I decided I would try to connect with Lady Zak Kuk, known as the Red Queen, who was said to have ruled Palenque eleven-hundred years before. I had been a student of Miguel Angel for a few years and felt a close connection with the Mayan Mother goddess, Ix Chel, whose wisdom came to me when I began working with him. I was very excited to connect with the Red Queen, as I'd discovered she was known for going into trance states and giving prophecy. As the early Mayan people had a profound connection with the mushrooms, I had a sense I would be able to reach her through them.

After our arrival at Palenque, I began searching for a quiet, hidden place where I could eat the gram of mushrooms I'd brought and hopefully reach her. I found a small pyramid off the beaten track and sat on a stair. I was wearing a large sunhat, sunglasses, and had brought a large container of water with me. I ate the mushrooms and waited. About twenty minutes later the spirit of a large black jaguar appeared and leapt over me, followed by an enormous bat that hovered in front of me and swiftly flew away. After that, a group of dark shapes with an ominous feel appeared before me. I was bound and determined to speak with the Red Queen and I spoke to this group with a stubborn authority, saying, "I'm here to speak to the Red Queen. I don't want any trouble." That is exactly what I told them and they moved off.

The next being to appear to me presented in an orange/red mist. It was the face and shoulders of a woman who wore a headdress of feathers, and between each feather was a serpent. The serpents were eyeing me as was the woman, and I knew they were reading my frequency. As I had done at other times in my journeys, I opened my heart in a gesture that revealed the entirety of my being. I knew in that moment that I was looking at the great Lady Zak Kuk. I opened the conversation with a question, asking, "Why is there still so much suffering in the world? Why? It breaks my heart." She replied, "The question is not *why*, the question is *how*. How do we heal this? It begins with gestures of kindness. Do not underestimate the power of a kindness to effect a change." As I had been deeply researching the nefarious actions of our so-called leaders and their hidden hands at that time, I replied, "I don't think the New World Order oligarchs are going to respond to a gesture of kindness. You need to realize what we're dealing with here." She replied, "It is not for them. It is the common people who are suffering and it is the common people who will respond to a gesture of kindness. You think nothing of making such a gesture yet you have no idea the gravity of its effects on another."

She went on to say, "Your world is run on fear. Your people have been taught to distrust. You distrust the nature of life, each other, even yourselves. So much so, that you discount the power of a kindness to affect a change in your world. You wouldn't recognize a deity if it was standing right before you!" Then she said, again, speaking to humanity in general, something that quite struck me, "You are nobility and you've forgotten." Our conversation continued and at one point she did something unexpected. The medicine that I work with as a practitioner is that of the owl, which is the ally of the seer. In my house I have a number of wings and talons from unfortunate birds found dead by the side of the road. They sit on various altars throughout my house.

The Red Queen plucked a feather from her headdress and extended her arm toward me, saying, "You are a collector of these." I reached out my hand and took the feather and as I drew it back, I felt doubt. I wondered in that moment if there was something connected to that feather because in everything there is some kind of exchange. I also wondered if this might be a trickster spirit and not the Red Queen. In that moment I respectfully handed back the feather and said, "I will be in my light, and you in yours." Immediately, I felt myself in a cylinder of crystal clarifying light and in that moment the realization hit me. THAT WAS THE RED QUEEN WHO GIFTED ME A FEATHER AND I GAVE IT BACK!! I was horrified and as soon as the realization came to me her words followed, "You have made your decision."

My eyes flew open and to my astonishment I saw that in my effort to find a quiet place I'd sat myself directly across from the only remaining face on the main pyramid situated further away in the center of the site. She spoke through the face and said, "Yes, it is I." Well, I'd brought offerings of cacao and fruit for her so I stood up and started walking to the pyramid to gift her, all the while bawling my eyes out, as I felt I'd failed miserably. Her voice came into my head saying, "Do not do this to yourself, we have spoken of so much and you will remember only this?" I climbed the stairs of the pyramid and walked around the face and gave my offerings to her. When I was finished, I put my hands over my heart and said, "I speak the language of the heart." Her response filled my eyes with tears. "As do we. As do we."

After descending the pyramid stairs, I began searching for Miguel Angel who I found at a little café on the site. He was sitting with the tour operator and the bus driver, both of whom were his students. With tears streaming down my cheeks, I explained what happened. My wise teacher, Miguel Angel, listened and said to me, "Perhaps you are not ready to carry the feather of a Mayan queen, Shonagh, and your inner wisdom knew that." He was right of course, and later that night I fell into an emotionally exhausted sleep. When I awoke the following morning the memory of what I'd done came back and I started crying again when her voice pierced through and said, "I knew you wouldn't take the feather! Now go home and write!"

I realized in that moment she had my number from the get-go. I always joke that your rap doesn't work in the spirit realms, they can see right into you. It was a test and Miguel Angel was right, I wasn't ready to carry the feather of a Mayan Queen, and it was not my place to. That is not the culture I was born into. I was deeply touched by that culture and its spirits taught me graciously. I knew though, that my time there was complete and when I left the Yucatan a few days later I knew I would never return.

Once home, I did more research and discovered to my utter astonishment that Lady Zak Kuk is always shown with a headdress of quetzal feathers. That not-so-minor detail eradicated any doubt I might have had as to whom I was speaking with at Palenque.

A few months after that I went into the mushroom realms where the spirits said to me, "Daughter, it is time for you to explore your own magical bloodline. You are a Celt." That was all they said and when I came out of that I began reading books on the gorgeous mythology and lore of the Celts and I was deeply moved. Having felt for the better part of my life like I was on the outside looking in, something deep in me felt restored, and for the first time ever, I had the sense of belonging, belonging to a culture I was only just starting to know.

A few months later I received an email from author, researcher, and public speaker, Freddy Silva, announcing a tour for just six people to the Outer Hebrides of Scotland to visit stone circles and other ancient sites. Freddy is also a photographer and his photos of the rural Scottish landscape and the dramatic, imposing stone structures took my breath away and I knew I had to go. In fact, I barely read the text other than the tour dates, as the images had such a visceral affect. I sent my deposit that day without hesitation.

Money was tight for me at that time and I saw the tour as a kind of pilgrimage. Sacrifice and dedication go hand in hand with a pilgrimage so I set my intention, called on the Fates, and worked like crazy and somehow it all came together. Serendipitously, I discovered one of my readers lived in Edinburgh and he invited me to stay with him and his wife for a couple of days before taking the train to Inverness where I rented a car, put on my big girl panties, and drove on the opposite side of the road all the way to the Isle of Skye, the most beautiful place I have ever been.

On Skye I stayed at a wondrously enchanting location in Dunvegan called Skye Eco Bells, a nine-acre off-grid campsite with colorfully-decorated cozy tents. I arrived at almost midnight and after settling myself, I sat on the steps outside my tent and looked up at the sea of stars. At that precise moment a comet with a fiery tail hurtled across the sky. I took that as a good omen.

My friend in Edinburgh had gifted me some wild mushrooms and though I had every desire to take them in that beautiful location it was not to be. I was 8 hours behind on Seattle time and had just a couple of days before I was to join Freddy's group. I was determined to get myself on Scotland time as I wanted to be fresh and present to every moment spent on that tour. The following day I drove to the Faerie Glen in Uig by Glen Conon. There, I was overwhelmed by the sweeping beauty of Balnaknock, the Faerie Glen. I spent the entire day wandering its lush green hills, soaking up the peaceful energy and basking in what felt like a mythic wonderland. It would have been a gorgeously magical setting for a light mushroom journey but I had to get back into that car and drive on the opposite side of the road. That experience will have to wait till I make my way back to Skye someday, hopefully with a friend who will do the driving.

I arrived at the hotel in bustling Glasgow where I would be meeting the other participants the following morning. The next day I awoke from a dream where a snake was seeking me. When I joined the group at the breakfast table, they were discussing snakes and the Druids of Ireland. This was the first of a number of unexpected synchronicities that occurred with regularity while on that extraordinary tour. I bonded with three of the women attendees who were highly intelligent, adventurous and very awake and aware. I was to learn much from these women moving forward, and a few years later they attended my small tour in Ireland that I co-led with woodland bard, John Willmott.

We boarded a small plane out of Glasgow to the Isle of Lewis which is home to the production of Harris tweed and host to a number of ancient stone circles, not the least of which is the great Callanish. While on the plane I settled into daydreaming when through my mind came a poetic message speaking to a key I was holding in my field and informing me that "the gates you'll stand before will yield." My understanding of the key in my field was that through the mushroom journeys I'd experienced to that point, my auric field had changed to reflect the changes in my mind state. I had definitely noticed my psychic abilities had been enhanced and that has continued to develop over the past several years of dedicated work with the mushroom teachers. My sense was that the key they spoke of would make me more sensitive to the energies in and around the stone circles. I would soon find out.

Let's first explore the deeper mysteries of these extraordinary stones.

Europe is home to numerous Neolithic stone circles that reflect astronomical movements in the sky. These circles perplexed 18th and 19th century archeologists who were of the prevailing belief that our 'rude ancestors' had no semblance of scientific astronomical understanding. Yet these ancient structures are mathematically precise in their placement. Their builders had a sophisticated grasp of astronomy, measure and number, arranging the stones to represent accurate astronomical cycles. This betrays a level of geometric skill and scientific understanding of landscape relative to the movements of the heavens that is staggering to consider when we think of their age. The study of this is called, 'Astro-archeology.'

In *Secrets of the Stones*, author, John Michell writes,

> "Resistance to astro-archeological theory has been intensified by the understanding that, if ancient people of Neolithic culture are credited with an astronomical science far in advance of medieval, and even in some respects of modern standards, current faith in the unique quality of our own scientific achievement is undermined."[34]

The orthodox beliefs of conventional archeology were eventually negated by the highly respected 19th century astronomer and scientist, Sir J. Norman Lockyer, founder and editor of the influential magazine, *Nature*. English-born Lockyer was an avid traveler and a keen observer of the landscape. In 1890 he vacationed in Greece where he became fascinated by the orientation of its ancient temples. In Europe, the old churches were customarily positioned to face the sunrise on the feast day of their patron saint. Lockyer speculated that Greek temples would follow a similar rule of placement. Further travels took him to Egypt and there he discovered that the temples were accurately positioned to face the rising and setting of certain planets at specific times of the year.

In 1894 he published a book titled, *The Dawn of Astronomy*, and he was rewarded for his efforts by vociferous condemnation from the archeologists of his day. His reply, simply, was his wish that every archeologist would at least learn a little astronomy.[35]

Later, he turned his attention to Stonehenge and other megalithic sites, publishing the book, *Stonehenge and Other British Stone Monuments Astronomically Considered* in 1906, and an expanded version three years later with further discoveries of the astronomical relationship of the structures and the geography of the landscape. In her book *Touchstones for Today*, geomancer Alanna Moore, writes,

> As at other megalithic sites studied, Lockyer noted that the earliest of megalithic sites (or the earliest parts of sites) marked the all-important festival dates on the cross-quarter days, the mid-points between the summer and winter solstice times that heralded the new seasons. These were at the beginning of February, May, August and November, and they were considered to be portal-like points of time of great mythic import. Lough Gur's Grange Circle has a stone avenue alignment to the early August Lughnasadh/Lammas festival, as well as to Samhain, in early November.
>
> At later sites, or in later reconstructions at existing sites, the emphasis had shifted more to the solar solstice dates, Lockyer found. This may well signify a shift from more Earth-based pagan religion to one of solar deity supremacy. It probably signified the arrival in the British Isles of the great sun god, Lugh, with a wave of immigrant Celtic people coming from the continent. Before those times, Goddesses ruled together with Gods and the Earth's fecundity was honoured as absolutely fundamental to life with Underworld forces pre-eminent.[36]

John Michell writes, "The science of the megalith builders was evidently of the magical variety, as practiced by the Chaldeans and studied by Pythagoras and the occult schools of Greece, a science whose aims and methods are still displayed in the native systems of geomancy in China, the East and Africa."[37]

To the Celts, rocks have long been known to possess a spiritual nature. They could house the spirits of the land or the spirits of ancestors, or hold intention or 'charge' put into them by a practitioner. They are also containers of power. It is thought that specific stones had a stabilizing effect on geopathic harmony. To disturb these stones by displacing or destroying them wreaked havoc among crops and animals. If returned to their original placement, harmony was restored to the area. In addition, certain stones were said to contain beneficial energies that would heal the sick, and the Celts believed there were stones that would make women fertile. John Michell wrote that, "It is recognized in traditionalist societies throughout the world that such rocks are receptacles of the vital spirit that animates nature."[38] An example of that statement is found in the Shinto religion where rocks are said to house a spirit the Japanese call, 'Kami'. Both the Celts and the Japanese regard stone as the dwelling places of spirits that radiate harmonizing energies affecting the growth of plants as well as health and wellbeing.

Philip Callahan, Ph.D., was born in Fort Benning, Georgia and joined the U.S. Air Force in 1943 where he worked as a radio technician. He was stationed in Ireland and while there he became keenly interested in the ancient round towers. At the base of the towers the grass was particularly verdant, which attracted Callahan's attention as he noticed that cattle and sheep preferred to graze around the perimeter of the towers. The animals were also partial to grazing within stone circles and close to megalithic structures. In examining the stone, he discovered it was paramagnetic. Callahan defines paramagnetism as "a strong positive attraction to a magnet. Most organic molecules are diamagnetic and most volcanic rock and ash are paramagnetic."[39] Diamagnetism is a weak opposition to a magnetic force. Paramagnetic stone attracts the electro-magnetic radiations from the atmosphere that are drawn to paramagnetic materials in soil and stone, which includes the stone used for the round towers, tombs and standing stones. When these energies meet, they create a harmonizing radiation that is taken up by the soil, benefiting soil health and plant growth. The standing stones and the stone towers of Ireland are functioning among other things, as natural antennae for the landscape.

As water is also diamagnetic it follows that plants which are mostly water, would be naturally attracted to paramagnetic stone.

During his station in Japan, Callahan became interested in traditional rock gardens and shrines, noting the shape of rocks used and their position in relation to the sun. This was not lost on him and he soon discovered,

> Interestingly enough, the spacing, and the horizontal and vertical proportions between the principle and subordinate rocks are often expressed according to the Golden Mean of the ancient Greeks. This tells us in no uncertain terms that antenna design, which is the shape and placement of the rocks operating as antennae in relationship to the sun, is of utmost importance. Among the gardens and shrines of Japan were found both paramagnetic and diamagnetic rocks. The ancient science of geomancy was used to select and site the stones, which were both male and female. The male stones were situated under direct sunlight while the female stones were placed in shaded, secluded areas. This tells us that geomancy has little to do with north and south pole magnetism, but in actuality, is a paramagnet/diamagnetic, or sun/shade phenomenon."[40]

Geomancy concerns the use of magnetic dowsing to select and site the stones. This practice originated in China and spread throughout the ancient world. In geomancy, rods known as 'divining rods' made of metal or a forked tree branch are held in the hands extended from the body. A question is asked and the rods or branch will respond by opening inward or outward or in the case of a forked branch, upward or downward. Pendulums are also used. A pendulum is a small weight like a stone or crystal suspended on a chain or string. This is commonly known as 'dowsing' and it has long been used to locate sources of water and metals as well as for 'placement surveyance' where dowsing of the landscape effectively determines the proper placement of a particular object such as a stone, the correct type of stone to use, etc. With dowsing you can search for anything, though to the uninitiated it sounds like pure bunk. We are electromagnetic beings living in an electromagnetic world and we can communicate with the landscape using our consciousness and our sensitivity and we can combine that with the pendulum or rods to receive answers to our queries.

The dowsers of old were high masters of geomancy and their knowledge was essential for the correct placement of sacred sites. John Michell wrote, "The flow of earth is affected by underground streams and veins of ore, and over these its intensified activity is apparent to those who can divine it. An earlier use for the dowser's sensitivity was in geomancy. A temple or shrine is obviously useless without a spirit to inhabit it, so its correct location relative to the natural paths and centres of the earth spirit was the first consideration of the ancient architects."[41]

We cannot underestimate the contribution by expert dowsers who have brought forth a wealth of important information on ancient stone structures throughout Europe. Dowsing has shown megalithic structures to be cited on or by magnetic lines of earth energy and in close proximity to water. In addition, dowsers who've tested the energies at the stones themselves have discovered electromagnetic currents of energy flowing forth from the stones and the structure as a whole. Some people have touched a standing stone and received a mild shock, which indicates these stones are holding a current. It has been discovered that these currents shift with the movements of the stars. In *The Secret Country* there is a story told by archeologist and dowser, T.C. Lethbridge, who published books on his experiments on stone circles using a pendulum. While dowsing to ascertain the age of the Merry Maidens stone circle in Cornwall he experienced the following:

> As soon as the pendulum started to swing, a strange thing happened. The hand resting on the stone received a strong tingling sensation like a mild electric shock and the pendulum itself shot out until it was circling nearly horizontally to the ground. The stone itself, which must have weighed over a ton, felt as if it were rocking and almost dancing about. This was quite alarming, but I stuck to my counting... The next day I sent my wife up alone to see what happened to her. She had the same experience. It has happened nowhere else. The Pipers were mute and so were many crosses and other monuments which I have tried. But most circular monuments are now incomplete and perhaps something has gone from them."[42]

Another interesting story was told by John Williams, an experienced dowser from Abergavenny, who put his hands on the stones and was flung back, recalling that a spiral-like force built up through his entire body as soon as he touched the stone, throwing him back from it. Another dowser and stone researcher, Andrew Davidson, gave a talk for the Lost Knowledge Organization in 1970, where he discussed the stone circle in Banffshire. "Through dowsing he found that each stone is predominately positive or negative and oppositely charged to its neighbor. There are polarity changes six days after the new moon, and on one such occasion he was dowsing at the circle and experienced the change. His pendulum slowly stopped, and then gained momentum in the opposite direction, the whole sequence taking seven minutes."[43]

Reginald Smith was the curator of British and Roman Antiquities at the British Museum. In 1939 he published a paper in the *Journal of the British Society of Dowsers* (vol.3) where he stated that all the ancient mounds and stone circles were positioned on centers of particularly strong current. Researcher, Freddy Silva, would refer to these centers as "geomagnetic hotspots."

I mentioned earlier that stones can be 'charged'. In his book, *Witches: Investigating an Ancient Religion*, archeologist and dowser, T.C. Lethbridge spoke to one of the possible functions of stone circles as accumulators of power. He wrote, "something from the human field can be fixed for long periods in the fields of various inanimate objects, including bits of stone. Apparently, the belief that power could be obtained by stepping up the current in human bodies is very old indeed. The stone circles, which are usually thought to be temples of some kind, are more probably places where violent dancing in a ring took place to engender power, much in the same way as in electricity, a moving coil generates power. The stones were probably put there with the idea of containing the power once it had been generated."[44]

If you have two opposing poles of a magnet and move a conductive wire through them it will generate an electric current. Janet and Colin Bord surmised that if you have a stone circle where each stone alternates between positive and negative charge and a group of dancers holding hands were to weave in and out of the stones they would be electrically connected, acting as a human conductive wire. They would effectively create a charge field that could be stored in the stones. As we are electromagnetic beings, that charge could have an effect on consciousness whereby the dancers could be put into an altered state where their awareness would be greatly enhanced.

The authors of *The Secret Country* wrote,

> The detailed surveying done by Professor Alexander Thom provides very positive indications that at least one function of stone circles was astronomical, but the precise calculations obtainable from these stone observatories were surely used for some purpose other than a farming calendar. It could be that the scientists of that age, by accurately plotting the positions and relationships in the heavens of the sun, moon, planets, and stars, could calculate the optimum time to capture and store the inflow of cosmic energies and the most favorable time for these energies to be released. If this should be so, then the stone circles had found mutually compatible purposes:
>
> 1. Astronomical calculators.
> 2. Generators of terrestrial energy.
> 3. Storage batteries for both cosmic and terrestrial energies.
> 4. Radiating devices to broadcast these energies across the land (possibly through the ley system).
>
> Naturally, constructions of stone were used because of the special qualities of this material, qualities which are absent from the more easily handled wood, made it eminently suitable for storage and transmission of power.[45]

The main stone used for the standing stones and circles is granite, which is hard and very durable. It also contains between twenty and forty-percent quartz, which is a piezo-electric crystalline mineral that when under pressure can produce an electric current. Janet and Colin Bord wrote, "When it is influenced by an electric field it will vibrate rapidly at frequencies measured in millions per second and is therefore used in resonators and oscillators for frequency control in electronic communications equipment."[46]

As a result of the energies accumulated in the stones, they have a rich history as healing agents. There are many stories in the British Isles and other parts of the world where people were healed of an ailment through direct contact with the stone. As well, certain highly charged stones were put into water to infuse it with the healing frequencies. The water would be imbibed and the patient would recover. In addition, dew was collected from known healing stones and taken as a therapeutic.

Certain stones healed specific ailments. For example, the holed stones found in the British Isles were said to be especially helpful for children. In Cornwall there is a very interesting stone called the Men-an-Tol, which is wheel-shaped with a two-foot diameter hole in the center. It sits between two standing stones that are on either side of the hole. This stone was said to have efficacy for the remediation of rheumatic illnesses. The afflicted individual would crawl through the hole in a ritual manner and one such ritual has the individual crawl through the hole nine times against the Sun. A child would be passed through the hole three times and then pulled three times along the grass in an easterly direction, while a sick infant would be passed through the hole from one mother to another.

Specific stones could be laid on or sat upon such as St. Fillan's Chair in Perthshire. On Dunfillan Hill part of the rock is shaped like a seat and it is from this place that St. Fillan blessed the community. This rock was said to offer a cure for rheumatism of the spine. Another stone seat, which remediates ague, (fever and chills), is located in Carmarthenshire situated next to the old church of Llangan. As so many churches are situated near wells and springs, this stone seat is located near the well of Ffynon Canna and goes by the name of Canna's Stone. The afflicted would first drink from the well then sit or sleep on the stone. This would be repeated for several days and sometimes weeks.

Stonehenge was said to hold tremendous healing properties. In his *History of the Kings of Britain*, Geoffrey of Monmouth quotes Merlin, saying,

> Laugh not so lightly, King, for not lightly are these words spoken.
> For in these stones is a mystery, and a healing virtue against many

ailments. Giants of old did carry them from the furthest ends of Africa and did set them up in Ireland what time they did inhabit therein. And unto this end they did it, that they might make them baths therein whensoever they ailed of any malady, for they did wash the stones and pour forth the water into the baths, whereby they that were sick were made whole. Moreover, they did mix confections of herbs with the water, whereby they that were wounded had healing, for not a stone is there that lacketh in virtue of leechcraft.[47]

Our ability to experience the subtle energies in these stones is because, like every living being on this Earth, we are electromagnetically charged. In Dr. Jerry Tennant's book, *Healing is Voltage*, he states that health and healing are possible primarily by the body's production of new cells. In order to be created, a new cell requires a *voltage* of -50 mV. As electrical beings we are affected by electrical frequencies whether they are naturally occurring or manmade. In Chapter One of *The Waves that Heal*, author, Mark Clement, illustrates this very clearly in his writing about Russian-born engineer and inventor, George Lakhovsky and his multi-wave oscillator, stating,

> The Fundamental principle of Lakhovsky's scientific system may be summed up in the axiom, 'Every living being emits radiation.' Guided by this principle Lakhovsky was able to explain such diverse phenomena as instinct in animals, migration in birds, health, disease, and, in general, all the manifestations of organic life. According to Lakhovsky the nucleus of a living cell may be compared to an electrical oscillating circuit. This nucleus consists of tubular filaments and chromosomes made up of insulating material and filled with a conducting fluid containing all the mineral salts found in sea water. These filaments constitute minute oscillating circuits endowed with capacity and inductance and capable of oscillating according to a specific frequency. They are comparable to the circuits, coils and windings of radio receivers.[48]

In an article from the December 1963 *Journal of Borderland Research*, a number of excerpts from Clement's book were commented on by the editor of the journal, Riley Hansard Crabb, who stated,

I believe Clement's comparison of a body cell with a radio receiver is only half true. The cell can also be compared with a radio transmitter when it is releasing energy. We are both radio-receptive and radio-active! Lakhovsky's theory should be acceptable to any occult scientist. The push-pull idea, the positive and the negative, the Law of Opposites, is basic to all forms and to all life at this level of existence. By inductance Clement means that radio-electricity can be induced or put into every cell of your body. By capacity he means that each body cell can hold a charge of radio-electricity, just as the battery of your car can carry a charge of electricity. In the case of your body, the charge is put in through invisible but very real radio waves. These can travel unimpeded through any solid object!

Having studied the work of George Lakhovsky and being the fortunate owner of his Multi-Wave Oscillator, I can understand now how a human being can have a heightened sensory experience within a charged stone circle or when in contact with a single charged stone. Our 'conducting fluid' as per Mark Clement's quote, carries a charge and can be charged by an outside influence.

Well, I did not have any of this knowledge when I set foot on the Isle of Lewis. I was there because I knew I had to be and I knew there was something waiting for me in this part of the world. In a way, it was good to go there so 'green', as I had no preconceived notions of what to expect. Our first day there was overcast, chilly and damp, typical weather for Scotland at that time. Prior to visiting Callanish Freddy took us to a small stone circle and before touching the stones I circumambulated the circle, then connected to a few of the stones. I then stood in the center of the circle and closed my eyes to feel the energy and that was when I 'felt' a tall male being on my left who extended his hand toward me, offering a gold sphere. I knew in coming to Scotland that I was among my people of the distant past and I reached out and took the sphere and placed it in my heart-center. I felt an immediate warmth emanating from that place and I felt like I had a device in there. After that, I began flowing poetry, no mushrooms needed, at almost every site we visited.

That this sphere was gold is significant, as gold relates to the Sun and the element of fire, both of which were highly regarded by the Celts for their sustaining power. The Sun symbolizes the light of knowledge, wisdom and understanding, and I have been seeking that for a great many years now and will continue for the rest of my life. And of course, I was soon to be told that it was a cauldron, and I explored that symbolism in great detail earlier in this book, and I continue to work with it today. Gold as a metal is highly conductive, symbolizing it as a means of communication, and it was said to have spiritual significance as a link to the supernatural world. Think of the symbolic gold ring or the grail cup. Many a story has been told of the shimmering, golden faerie realms and their cups and jewels of gold and silver.

We were able to visit Callanish twice and had the time to wander the site and experience the impossibly tall and regal stones. It was at Callanish where the first poetic transmissions came through as I pressed my body into the tall center stone. Knowing to bring my recorder I took it out of my pocket when I felt the words come in and spoke my poetic dialogue with the stone into the microphone. Throughout the rest of the trip as we visited each ancient site, I continued to receive poetic messages that I dutifully recorded.

The spirits of ancient Scotland opened my heart in such a way that I will forever hold the mystery of that land with the deepest reverence and also longing. It is my hope to visit the Orkneys someday, as the Ring of Brodgar and the Standing Stones of Stenness are also calling to me. Though I have no relatives who live in Scotland, it feels like home, and the father of my daughters is a descendent of the Home Clan of Scotland and both my daughters attended Saint Andrews University.

I was gifted poetry by the spirits of the stones, with the ability to communicate with them at certain times, and I am humbly grateful for that. It is my hope that some of what I share here will touch and inspire you, dear reader.

Scotland's Call

I'm called to Scotland's mists and green
To places where the Fae are seen
I'll camp outside beneath the stars
And enter realms at certain hours
Where portals grand will open wide

And Fae will bother not to hide
Their faces from my awestruck stare
But rather they will sit and share
Great secrets kept until this day
When humbly, I will visit Fae

A pilgrimage that I must make
For at this time, so much at stake
The moment's come to wake the crowd
The Faerie folk are getting loud
In order that they break the spell
That keeps Earth's people in a hell

And holds them on a hamster wheel
A corporate mindset that conceals
The magic that has never left
So many people are bereft

They dearly yearn for something more
But cannot find an open door
That takes them to a higher floor
Where they can alter what's in store
If mankind sleeps this dreamless sleep
That limits us to hapless sheep

The world of Nature begs our call
And though one person may feel small
One by one becomes most all

And then Earth's people will not fall
As we put forth a noble plan
To raise the consciousness of man

This endeavor begins with sight
Illuminating the dark of night
That lifts the ignorance of the masses
And gifts them with a pair of glasses
Of which the lens offers quite a view
Of possible outcome when more than a few
Of Earth's good people can see through

The machinations of hate and deceit
Put forth by those of great conceit
Who underestimate Earth's folk
And think that they can easily stoke
The fires of manipulation
Within people throughout nations
Who are glued to TV-set
Seduced by spells they do not get
But this game isn't over yet

As more folk look to Elf and Fae
A partnership from older days
Will rekindle in the hearts of man
And magic will return and span
The farthest reaches of this Earth
When men and women both will birth
A kinder and a wiser station
With the blessed cooperation
Of the folk of Faerie nations

This, my vision quest and prayer
As I climb the ancient stairs
And so, to Scotland green, I go
To seed my vision that I'll sow

And If I'm gone without a trace
You'll know I've joined the Faerie race
To work from realms unseen by most
With beings from a different coast

Adventure and great mystery
Are waiting patiently for me
To visit ancient glens afar
Where Fae await the magic hour
When veils are thin and mists are clear
That is when this ancient seer
Will reach out with extended hand
To bond once more with ancient band
Of shimmering beings of wonder and grace
Who've long captivated the human race

Green glens and moors, I'll be there soon
To dance beneath September's Moon
Where my good heart will surely swoon
As Fae and Elf perform their tune...

Message on the Plane to Isle of Lewis

Be with self in clear mind now
When you come we'll teach you how
To use the key you hold inside
The faerie stallion you will ride

You've been marked within your field
The gates you'll stand before will yield
Your good heart will take you far
As we walk with you in this hour

Trust the timing, daughter dear
You are led by ancient seers
We know that you feel alone
We'll guide you to ancient stone
Where you will make a wish with power
That brings good fortune to this hour

Happiness will be your prize
As those tears fall from your eyes
Yes, we love you, daughter dear
You, once gifted ancient seer

Watch for signs along the way
That we'll put forth during your stay
Yes, the snake is seeking you
Ancient wisdom known to few

You'll step through the secret door
After which you'll know far more...

Prayer to the Stones at Callanish

This breath of fire I give thee
Offering my heart openly
Passing life force to and fro
Within this sacred stone I go

Open, please, your door to me
My heart bare, so you can see
Asking with humility
For the gift of sight to see

The seer's gift I ask of you
I promise I will hold it true
Like I once did so long ago
Once again these seeds I'll sow

Though I have no memory
Of what this mute place used to be
Still I feel it in my bones
Something tells me I am home

As I hold this stone so tight
I can feel the circle's might
Holding magic that is bright
Here for us in this dark night

I call in the Sidhe today
Asking now for light to stay
I call the Watchers who are kin
Open this door, please let me in

Confer to me your wisdom, clear
I will receive with open ear
This, my request of ancient seer
Who for too long has shed such tears

I pray this world awakens now
I know you have the knowledge how
It comes to pass and so I ask
Bring day to night so we can bask
In wisdom once again on Earth
This vision now I ask to birth

And feel my gratitude in hand
For bonding me to shimmering band
Of Elfin and Fae who brighten my day
And mold my heart like wetted clay
And so dear ones I'm finally here
Standing tall with nary a fear

Woman's breath of fire blows
Through ancient stone whose wisdom sows
The mystery of infinite knowledge
Here I stand at ancient college
Humbly here with open heart
I pray, I ask you help me start
A life of happiness and joy
Let's heal Earth rather than destroy...

Answer From the Stones

We stand here now in modern day
And what would seem so far away
Is reunited with you here
As you stand among the seers
Watchers here who love you so
Take our wisdom so you'll know
How to walk upon the Earth
For at this time there is a dearth
Of good seers and Earth keepers...

Callanish

The day I stood at Callanish
The heavy clouds held sway
While stones stood tall and glorious
Against the looming gray

I walked three counter circles 'round
About the central space
Where high initiates once stood
I humbly showed my face

I broached the tallest central stone
Slowly and with care
And leaned into its rocky face
My soul I did lay bare

Then from the ground beneath my feet
A subtle current flowed
Up through my legs and then my spine
Till in my head it glowed

A taste of nectar on my tongue
A gift from ancients so far-flung
Yet present in that moment, rare
I kissed the stone, 'twas only fair

And that was when the Sun peeked out
The clouds, they gently parted
And stone and I were light throughout
I knew not what I'd started

I only know that Callanish holds magic in its stones
And in the ground beneath the place
A kind of cosmic phone
Was activated long ago

By beings who were in the know
Tis in this place a soul can grow

Initiates can be bestowed
The light of wisdom then can ground
And heaven truly can be found
By opening an inner door
Within the stone and beneath floor

And also in initiate's heart
This door will then reveal the art
Of crafting spells that tap the well
Of knowledge leading out of hell
Unto a place the ancients knew
Known now only to a few

And so, I hold this story dear
Since Callanish my mind's been clear
In my mind there's now a well
I can feel its waters swell

"Make a wish," it says to me
"I'm your gift that helps you see
You can tap the mysteries
And travel down the ancient tree
To reach below where we will show
The answers that you seek to know..."

In the Tree

Called to sit within this tree
A throne of wood and greenery
Surrounds me here by fleur-de-lis
Upon a chapel by the sea

The tree branch calmly eyes my face
While I receive its earthly grace
Dear spirit of this tree, do share
What secrets you have hidden there

I close my eyes and hold tree stalk
In hopes I'll hear the spirit talk
Then up above, sweet sound of bird

In perfect timing, greetings heard
The wind then rustles through the leaves
When something whispers, "Dear, believe"

"Sit quietly and hear us out
The elementals here have clout.
The key you seek is hidden still
But you are on a path of will
That calls you to the mystery
That you know is no fantasy.

Men of grace have blessed this place
To counter the curse on the human race
The spirits here do not cause fear
What you must shed, we will help clear
This path you walk it slowly builds
As each step brings you closer still... "

Message from the Sidhe

Those who come before you stand
As emissaries from a land
That most today think nothing of
Yet we, the people of the dove
Shower you with blessings, gay
You are speaking to the Fae

Together, we have opened wide
The secret door that lives inside
You have seen it, this we know
From this moment you will flow
Our wisdom and our conversation
Through the medium of your nation

Can you feel it, daughter dear
As we whisper in your ear?
Once again you play the seer
Call to us, we're always near

"You are getting," as we say
The spell of ignorance you'll slay
To the great queen we have come
You, a daughter of the Sun

You will end small-minded worry
Tis the time for you to hurry
See dear one, the spell is lifted
Feel the cauldron you've been gifted

Where it sits in your heart-center
This, the place through which we'll enter
Practice turning up the flame
You will not feel quite the same

We will teach you how to use
This magic sphere you won't abuse
Use the vision in your mind
And with the sphere you will combine
The power of imagination
With this flame within your nation

Weave a vision for this Earth
That brings your kin back home to birth
A magic that they cannot quell
For waters rising from this well
Will drown the sorcerer's mythic curse
They will leave here in a hearse

See it daughter, call it in
At this time we will surely win
Spread your wisdom far and wide
Don't play small, you must not hide

Your poetry will charm the many
We'll see that you won't lack for any
Earthly care you feel you need
We present you with a steed
Of sorts you'll ride to where
You wish to take your grand affair

See it now within your mind
Dear, you are no longer blind
Play an inner harmony
That activates the energies
Send it throughout all your cells
This will keep your body well

Call in the flute you seek to play
You will learn from we, the Fae
'Twill be just like yesterday

With fingers light and breath, you slayed
And cast your good spells on the crowd
Dear, you made us very proud

And so again you wish to play
The faerie flute of yesterday?
Then to you comes a magic wand
A flute so fine that it will bond
Quite nicely with your magic prose
You will touch them to their toes

Feed your folk this nectar, sweet
What you share will aptly treat
The malaise of modern man
We will help you so you can
Carry forward so much magic
To best counter all the tragic
Suffering of Earth's good folk
Use your power to invoke

Your gifts of humor and words, wise
Those you teach can realize
The magic well they hold within
We will get beneath their skin

And activate the ancient codes
In DNA where stories told
Will start to pierce forgotten veil
Where deep inside, the Holy Grail
Lies waiting to sing once again
Upon this thirsting earthly plane

Do not succumb to sorcerer's spell
That seeks to rob the sacred well
And rape the lady of the Sidhe
Who guards it for eternity

We choose carefully, you know
You are ready now to sow
The seeds you've trained to hold with care
Now you'll cast them everywhere

We're seeding minds here at this time
You can do it with your rhymes
As well, your wisdom shared with grace
You'll sprout magic in this place

And so, get ready for a ride
That brings good fortune to your side
Upon your face we look with pride
As we deliver a new tide

What you see will change markedly
As Earth begins to wrestle free
From all the pressure put upon her
She'll unleash a kind of monster
That unexpectedly will throw
A wrench into their spell of woe
That has been cast upon this place
By beings of a different race

Yes, dear, Earth is quite the place
To beings from a different space
Who care not for this sacred land
But rather take you by the hand
To lead you to your own destruction
Now the Earth can barely function

It will take catastrophe
For the sleeping ones to see
But know, dear, if it comes, that we
The Shining Ones you call, the Sidhe
Will keep you safe eternally
And you will walk this earthly plane
With the Shining Ones again...

Faerie Flute

It may feel unfamiliar now
But if you practice you'll know how
To fill the air with wondrous song
Trust us dear, it won't take long
Before you're playing many tunes
That you will play beneath the Moon

And we'll come forth to welcome you
To worlds known only to a few
Who know inside, the notes to play
That bring you face-to-face with Fae

Know that you will deftly play
Enchanting tunes from yesterday
You'll play in both worlds expertly
Guided by your kin, the Sidhe

Take your time and learn it well
And with your poetry you'll tell
The stories told from earlier times
That you'll express with clever rhymes

This is quite the combination
Ushered through imagination
In your hand a musical wand
That will take your words beyond
The gateway to the human heart
This, the magic of the smart

Who see a different avenue
Through which to reach a select few
Who'll activate their own devices
Peppering the Earth with spices
That will flavor cauldron's stew
To feed the souls of more than few

Oh, dear daughter here we go
Cards held in hand we will soon show
Meanwhile, you will learn to play
A magic flute that calls in day
To end this dark night you've been in
Comes now the light that lives within
The hearts of man, our blessed kin
A new mindset we will begin...

The Cauldron

Dear, we won't let you forget
Rest assured that we will whet
Your appetite to know far more
You've only just opened the door
To everything that's come before

It will come through revelations
Stirring life within your nation
Stay the course with your good ship
Soon the wisdom from your lips
Will bare the mark of one who knows
The cauldron's fire in you grows

Stoke it well and use the breath
Energize that center with
The visionary thoughts in mind
We are offering you kind
Advice to help you to awake
For at this time so much at stake...

Incantation

I stoke the flames of cauldron here
I know will help this ancient seer
To see with inner eye that's clear
And help me well, my ship to steer...

Cauldron Alchemy

Don't forget the cauldron, fine
Use the power of your mind
In the morn, before you rise
See it with your inner eye

Tend the fires of this bowl
Strength of focus is your goal
Feel the warmth in your heart center
Feel the presence of your mentors

This, the portal we come through
Here so we can speak with you
You stood with extended hand
And we, etheric shimmering band
Of old friends answered, now we're here
To break the spells and help you clear
The detritus within your mind
That clouds the thinking of your kind

This takes practice everyday
Repetition is the way
Your media repeats constantly
But our spells are designed to free
Your mind from imposed limitations
Stifling you within your nation

Now back to that cauldron, old
Inside heart center it burns bold
Send its light out like a beacon
When you wish to be a speakin'
With the wisdom keepers, we
You can feel us in the trees

And as well in circles old

Come to us, we will unfold
The secret teachings hidden here
Technologies designed to clear
And also strengthen your heart's light
So you can see in this dark night

What's put in cauldron hot, is changed
Information is exchanged
And as it is rearranged
What started out a certain way
Now puts on a new display

A carefully planned recipe
Initiates the alchemy
The right ingredients help you see
Your mind provides the recipe

It's like a cabinet where the meat
And the bitter and the sour
And the honey from the flower
Can be found to spike the brew
The magic's found inside of you

And so, retrain your mind, you must
And with a fiery heart you'll bust
The bubble you've been trapped within
You'll see right through the sorcerer's spin
And that's the moment you'll begin
To tip the scales so Earth can win
Her precious children's good minds back
That for so long have been attacked

The cauldron centered in your chest
Draws out from you the very best
Intentioned actions made with care
Informed by wisdom with its flair

For accessing the sacred stairs
That lead into the hidden lair

Where teachers of the mystery
Will help you walk with eyes to see
And ears that hear the reverie
Of Nature's songs that magically
Inspire creativity
Within the temple of your mind
Combined with heart's fire, you'll design
An entirely different way
To walk the path you walk today

You must cast all self-doubt away
Stand in your power, do not sway
Still yourself to hear our words
We will speak through tree and bird
And wind and water and the green
And the skies above you seen

You, a child of Earth and Star
Have incarnated at this hour
To birth a magic once known well
It will transform this current hell

But first, the inner alchemy
Through cauldron heart and mind you'll free
Yourself from chronic thinking habit
Which takes you, like Alice's rabbit
Down that famous hole, confusing
Deliberately diverting musings
That could solve so many things

Take from us the golden ring
That stills the mind and stokes the heart
This, the first place where you start

To activate the changes needed
In your minds is where we've seeded
With our clever charming rhymes
Treasures for these troubled times

Now the ball is in your court
Sit in silence and then sort
Like laundry, separate dark from light
See it all, do not feel fright
Then pick and choose what will be cleaned
As you create a different scene...

Grace

Grace is the spell that I now cast
I have raised this vessel's mast
Through the dark night I have walked
To the light that I have stalked

To the shores of Watchers, kind
I have anchored in my mind
The treasure of my magi self
I hear clearly Fae and Elf
Voices sweet and wisdom, sure
This is where I find the cure
To the delusions of this maze
I now let go of that phase

And humbly enter hallowed halls
Where the snowy white owl calls
Me to the rings of ancient stones
Where I feel deep inside my bones

An internal activation
In the depths of my soul's nation
I hold now a gifted key
That enables me to free

Myself from thoughts of limitation
I've arrived at a new station
"Daughter of 3 Mothers," I
When I heard those words, I cried
Venus, Danu, Brighid, fair
I did climb the ancient stairs

Whereupon gates opened wide
And I saw standing by my side
Shimmering beings tall and white
Assisting me to stem the blight

Of my own ignorance of knowledge
They took me to an ancient college
This one takes a while to find
For it lies hidden in the mind

This journey truly is within
The key is here beneath my skin
A golden sphere my heart now holds
I stand as initiate, bold
In this world though I'm not of it
What a journey, how I love it
Flanked by ancient kin so wise
They have gifted me new eyes
To see beyond the same old story
To a place of mythic glory

A new chapter has begun
Its seeds nurtured by the Sun
My sojourn continues on
As I welcome a new dawn...

Farewell Sweet Scotland

Farewell sweet Scotland
Land so green
Your ancient circles I have seen
Filled with grace, I've stood between
Both worlds while flanked by shining beings

Oh, dear Scotland, I will yearn
Within my heart a fire burns
A gold light given me that day
By a member of the Fae

Who placed it in my trusting hand
That touched my heart so it could land
And cast its glow inside of me
Where it will live eternally

Oh, Scotland fair, a living temple
You have given more than ample
Messages from those long passed
Who have left behind a vast
Treasure trove of mystery, old
Captivating we, the bold

Initiates who've come before
Incarnate now to settle score
To weave the magic back again
On this ancient earthly plane

Scotland green, you hold the keys
That unlock many mysteries
I leave for now but will return
To sit in circles where I'll learn
In ways that are not recognized
Most modern folk do not have eyes

To see into your libraries
And open to your mysteries

Scotland dear, you hold such beauty
Glens to shores, a pirate's booty
Everywhere I look I'm awed
Your landscape is a gift from God

From Skye to Mull to Iona's shores
Each place has opened many doors
Within my aching heart that longs
To hear the morning magpie's songs

Dear Scotland old, you're in me now
And I will figure a way how
To land upon your shores again
In my future, there's a plane
With wings to take me back to you
To soak up green and skies of blue
To sit in Faerie rings of old
To feel the mystery unfold
Oh, Scotland green, my soul is stirred
I pray this poetry is heard
By those within your circles round
Because of them my soul, I've found
I leave today forever changed
My thinking process, rearranged

Such gratitude for this rare chance
Oh, Scotland, I'll be back to dance
Upon your green glens and your shores
And breathe the air of windy moors
Until that time, I bow to thee
Because of you, my heart's now free...

Move Forward

More to be revealed, they say
As you finish up your stay
Here on Earth, your story's laid
Daughter, do not be afraid.

For we've written a closing chapter
That will live on for years after
You have left this place behind
Daughter, your spells are the kind
That open hearts and stir the soul
Now's the chance to become whole

To call the magic back again
To this ancient earthly plane.
You've the power in your prose
You, we call, "Daughter Who Knows"

Speak your magic poetry
That invites your folk to see
Through the mists of man's deceptions
Raise the veil for the inception.
A return of wisdom, old
Delivering you from the cold
Into the warmth of truth and knowledge
Cleave yourself to this great college

You'll be led and guided there
What you learn you will then share
Though some may jeer and at you, stare
You hold the light now in your heart
Welcome to a brand-new start...

The Riders of the Sidhe, John Duncan, 1911.
(Dundee Art Galleries and Museums Collection.)

Post Scotland Magic

How beautiful they are,
The Lordly Ones,
Who dwell in the Hills,
In the Hollow Hills.

– The Immortal Hour, Fiona Macleod

Having immersed myself in the electromagnetic fields of the Scottish stone circles and other magical sites, I felt like I was pulsating with that energy, and I was. On the plane from Glasgow to my connection in Chicago, I poured forth poetry for seven hours. I was seated next to a Scottish couple and at one point the husband looked over to me and exclaimed, "Are ya writin' a book over there or what? Ya haven't stopped since we took off!"

After a couple of days back home I had a distinct sense that the Sidhe had traveled with me to my cottage in Redmond. I could feel their presence in my field and I decided to do an experiment. I sat down in front of my computer and opened up a word document. I put my hands on the keyboard and waited. Not one minute later poetry came flowing through me like warm honey, and the most delightful, funny and kindly message came forth that had me laughing out loud. They felt like dear old friends, confidantes and advisors. I did not know if they would speak to me again, and even today after all these years where they have graced me with their wisdom many times over, I never presume they will automatically come through and talk to me. I am always awed and deeply grateful to receive their words.

For the next three months they consistently flowed their messages through me. Most often, the messages came as I was just waking up to the outer world, but still with a foot in the pool of dreams. I was in that liminal in-between state, which is amenable to receiving telepathic transmissions and claircognizant knowing. In would come poetic words and I would snap awake, realizing this was happening in real time and I needed to grab my recorder to take dictation. It got to the point where I would bring my digital recorder to bed with me, keeping it at the ready by my pillow.

Two particularly lengthy messages came through over that time, one of which flowed in as I was preparing breakfast for my daughter. I had to drive her to school and so I asked the Sidhe if they could wait until I got back home to finish their message, and the words promptly ceased. When I returned home and closed the door behind me the words continued where they left off and the transmission completed itself. One of those transmissions, *Stone Circle Whispers*, came through with tremendous force and its message continues to captivate me to this day.

Transmissions came in for friends I knew over that time and I have shared two of those messages in this series. One is a message for the man who was my first mentor in the study of Natural Law over ten years ago, and I am eternally grateful to him for instilling in me a deep appreciation for the timeless maxims of law that have been an exceptional source of navigation and empowerment for me ever since. The second transmission was for a friend who was about to go through a divorce. How many of us have felt the sadness, grief, fear and anxiety of knowing a marriage or serious relationship was at the end of its time? I feel that message for her can extend to others for whom those words may be a comfort.

The Shining Ones who so generously give me these words are immensely kind and their messages penetrate with gentleness and humor. And yet, they are not trifling little Tinkerbells. They convey wise counsel and when needed, they can scold with a level of true caring that is felt through the weave of their words. Stern advice can indeed be given without shaming and reprimanding, and at the same time, without coddling either. I have been the recipient of that, in particular, because of my addiction to that demon-spawn, sugar, which they are decidedly disapproving of. As well, they have spoken in no uncertain terms to my tendency to doubt myself and my preference to play small and avoid a larger playing field.

A number of transmissions in this series place emphasis on the power of the mind and I can assure you, they have been drumming into my thick Aries skull that how I think determines my experiences and what I attract to myself. For the first three years of my mushroom forays the emphasis was on "get your mind right, dear." In fact, I heard that admonition both while on and off the mushroom and I understood that I had to do major clean-up in the great halls of my mind. It wasn't until I did the heavy lifting there that they then began to show me how to tap the magical power of my mind. The mind is a temple and one must keep a temple clean or the treasure held there becomes almost impossible to find with all the clutter of belief systems, cultural conditioning, programming, past hurts and traumas, etc.

The transmissions in the latter part of this next series emphasize the magical nature of the mind and how to work with it. This messaging continues on through the book, as if to consistently remind us that in truth we are magis, and we must break the spells of our conditioning that have been imposed on us everywhere we turn today. Poetry has the power to both cast a spell and break a spell and it is through this magical-speak that the spirits of Nature call us back to ourselves.

Message from the Fae on Thursday

Tired daughter, sitting here
Tired daughter, listen clear
No more machinations, bad
We wish now to see you glad

You have opened up the door
Let's give you a little tour
Of what's inside and what's in store
Then you'll be hungry for more

You have deep within your chest
Technology designed to wrest
You from the cult of mass delusion
We have gifted a solution

Use that mind of yours so sharp
Play it like a fine-tuned harp
Don't spend time on spells of worry
Leave aside that wretched slurry
Walk through thresholds made of green
You have tapped this, sight unseen
Trusting that we'd take you there
Now do your part, it's only fair

Break that habit, you old nun!
Dear, it's time to have some fun
Use the wand, imagination
Use the will within your nation

Weave a vision that brings laughter
See beyond into hereafter
We'll ensure you get this piece
This is like the Golden Fleece

Train your mind, dear, like before
Know you've opened up the door
This, the door that gets you out
You are packing major clout

You can walk right out of here
Into lands where minds are clear
Focus now upon your vision
It's not unlike wild sport fishin'

Where you must keep rod in hand
And make sure that you steady, stand
So when that big fish takes the bait
You had the patience there to wait

With your eyes upon the sea
Soon a success you will be
Holding in your hand the catch
That you worked so hard to snatch
You're in a new training now
We've come with you to teach you how
To use that cauldron in heart center
Think of us as your new mentor

We'll continue with these rhymes
We've helped you at other times
And you got it, daughter, dear
You, once gifted ancient seer

This you've asked for once again
On this ancient earthly plane
So dear, use imagination
Potent wand within your nation

Visualize daily what you wish
Then wait until you hook that fish!

It can be this easy, true
No more you'll doubt, it weakens you

If we appeared before you now
Daughter, you would have a cow
We'll continue in this way
Weaving rhymes throughout the day

Worry not, we'll let you sleep
At that time, we won't make a peep
How we love to hear your laughter
Wait until you see what's after

Oh, he's coming closer now
Though you often wonder how
That's for us to weave with ease
We will simply ask you, please

To keep your focus on this work
Practice daily, it won't hurt
Keep your mind trained expertly
In this way you'll ensure you're free

From the spells cast on your race
You are learning a new pace
From which to create in this hour
You are accessing your power

Others, they doubt and complain
Don't fall prey to their refrain
Work your magic with your friends
Help them bring this to an end

No more they'll struggle to believe
But rather have it up their sleeve
And cast their spells like magis, old

Once they get it, they'll be bold

Dear know, the cat's out of the bag
This, the wisdom of the hag
Who they once burned and tortured, cruel
We will see who is the fool
Who thinks they'll get away with murder
Justice finds the ones who've burned her

Make your dinner for your girls
We will wait to cast more pearls
In the meantime, think of flute
That temporarily is mute

On its way to your sweet lips
This will be a whole new trip
You will practice everyday
With your teachers, we the Fae

Wait until you hear that sound
You'll be jumping up and down
How your laughter pleases us
We can feel you start to trust

Tonight, dear, you'll sleep so fine
No more stories in that mind
Let it rest, we'll clear the way
Hold us close, your kin the Fae...

Message for a Friend

Daughter of the green isles, fair
We wish you now to be aware
This initiation you'll begin
Will make you strong within your skin

Cutting ties in a kind way
Though it hurts you both to say
That endings come, and when they do
Within your hearts you'll start to brew

A new life, one that calls to you
That cannot gift you till you're through
You will be supported here
By many folk who will be near

And far as well, for you've got kin
Who'll stick with you through thick and thin
Dear, a wondrous world awaits you
Take this chance, the gates you'll walk through

When you do, you'll realize
And we'll see wisdom in your eyes
Because you'll see you've got the chops
And, dear, we'll pull out all the stops

To call you from your comfort zone
And give you time to be alone
To get to know the woman, wise
Who lives in you, though you disguise
Her sometimes when you hide behind
Others who are actually blind

You must learn to trust yourself
We invite you, Fae and Elf

To call us to your inner temple
That is where we'll give you ample
Education like old times
Piercing veils with clever rhymes

You came here to dispense magic
You came here to quell the tragic
Loss of memory of connection
You, dear one, are an injection

Medicine, you are for many
Call us in, we'll give you any
Guidance that you need today
You, who once channeled the Fae

Get your business taken care of
We'll ensure you get your share of
All you'll need to live your life
You will not experience strife

Trust, dear one, we have your back
Walk this path and you won't lack
For anything you think you'll need
It is time to plant new seeds

So dear daughter of isles, green
We say now you have been seen
As you stood in circles, old
Remembering what you'd been told
Lifetimes ago when there you stood
A young priestess who knew she would
Return again to circles, magic
At a time when there was tragic
Damage done to Mother Earth
You would come back here to birth
A new example how to be
With your innate creativity

And so, there's more you're meant to do
We'll reveal it all for you
But first take care and cut the tie
Know that there's a time to die
Beyond death, you'll begin anew
To walk the path that's asked of you
Pain you'll feel but you'll move on
To greet with trust the coming dawn...

Old Spirits Speak

That's exactly what they fear of
That you realize what you're made of

The construct is a sorcerer's spell
Designed by those who know full well
The power of their words of art
They can initiate the start
Of any trend that they design
To keep the flock they watch in line
Change will come when minds start opening
Then the dawn of what you're hoping
Will ensue to shift the pace
This death march by the human race
Must be reversed, that's why we're here
Deception's mists we pledge to clear

Each of you has been assigned
A role you'll play to realign
The threads that weave this current hell
Your actions here will fare quite well
To shift the subtle frequencies
So more Earth folk begin to see
With inner eye to realize
The tricks by those who are disguised
As well-known personalities
Who manipulate the crowd with ease

This, dears, is a hologram
And we deliver telegram
That though the claws have dug in deep
And though the masses are asleep
A vow was made far in the past
That at this time we'd raise our mast
And sail into the stormy sea

To raise our great humanity
To heights once thought impossibly
Ambitious for such undertaking
Yes, this has been most painstaking
Though right now more of you waking
This the time we've been awaiting

See their fear, all that surveillance?
See the one world dark alliance?
They are under the impression
They're above divisive action
Which they spread among the crowd
Kept divided, lost and proud

But they cannot control each other
They are going to have one mother
Of a vast rift all among
The web of lies that they have strung
This, dears, we've been counting on

In the meantime, spread your song
Of what can be when hearts are strong
And minds are clear to urge along
The many who are so confused
Their precious souls have been abused

And so, the magic that you carry
Isn't simply airy-fairy
This, dear, has for long been crafted
By the lifetimes you've enacted

Now's your moment, all of you
We will give more than a few
Instructions clever, that you'll use
To take your folk beyond this ruse

Never let your good hearts waver
In those temples lives the savior
You, awakened ones of light
Illuminating this dark night
And gathering once more to cast
A spell you've trained for that has vast
Effects upon this sacred place
That's home to many kinds of race

Wake now, all, the gateway's open
Here's the moment you've been hoping
Will occur on planet Earth
Songs were written of this birth
That springs forth from within the mind
A realization of the kind
That halts the course dramatically
When of a sudden, people see

This thing's electric, think how fast
When switch is flicked the light is cast
And everything you didn't see
Is now before you quite clearly

Oh, many changes coming near
Children of the light, don't fear
But rather sing your gifts with joy
And with good wisdom you'll destroy
The spell that captivates the many
What you carry conquers any
Thing they've up their sleeve
You simply in your mind conceive
Of what you were before you came
And when you realize you're the same
Well, dears, consider that in mind
An ancient spell you will unbind

For the great wand of antiquity
Is buried where you cannot see
For you've been taught to look outside
And not within where it resides

You are ready now to find
The Holy Grail within your minds
The sacred places you have been
Hold keys there that remain unseen
Unless you've trained for many lives
To cut through darkness with your knives

Those swords of light you hold with grace
Look in the mirror at your face
Look in your eyes that dance their light
You, a warrior here to fight
A battle that is ancient old
And now the time of stories told
When beauty beings fair and tall
Will once again appear to all
And help you, dear ones, at this time
Heed the power of this rhyme

For this is just the start of things
As people of the faerie rings
Cast their magic spells around
So once more earthly folk can found
A time of peace upon this Earth
A time when your good folk can birth
The frequencies of living grace
Whose energies will heal this place...

Stone-Circle Whispers

The great stones that make circles, round
Strategically placed upon the ground
Beneath the ground the circuitry
Of Earth's magnetics you can't see

Then there is geometry
Within the stones, again unseen
The math creates a frequency
A vortex that will help you see

A layering of energies
Found too, in sacred groves of trees
The stones, like trees, are quite alive
Programmed by wise folk who did strive
To create earthly libraries
For those seeking the mysteries

And in these circles are vibrations
That are felt within your nation
Designed to raise your frequency
And open your third-eye to see

A kind of prehistoric phone
So that you'll know you're not alone
For these designs will blow the mind
The architects of these great finds
Gained access to colleges in the stars
From which they were given special powers

These architects knew someday the hour
Of ignorance, would thoroughly scour
The Earth, whose good folk would be slaves
Subject to false leaders, depraved

Long past unwritten history
Initiates of the mystery
Could see far-flung of what's to come
The voices of the cycles sung

And so preparing for the fall
Great stones were placed in ways that call
Inviting folk to stand within
A circle, round where they'd begin
To understand technologies
Designed to open eyes to see

These great stones hold the energy
That long was placed by wise ones, we
The Shining Ones you call the Sidhe
The knowledge here will set you free

Allow us to take up your time
With this very simple rhyme
We are an electric current
Flowing throughout time and space
When you activate in circles
You can take us any place

For those great circles were designed
To activate us in your mind
Initiates stood in circle's center
Calling in the ancient mentors

If you've prepared with heart, mind ready
If you stand there tall and steady
If you're humble and receptive
We can give you your directive

You can tap your ancient lifetimes
We provide a kind of lifeline

Here for folk at any time
A pilgrimage to realign
And speak with ancestors, divine

The great stones may look old and battered
We will say it doesn't matter
Set in stone we once did cast
These places hold the knowledge, vast

To those who come with right intention
We'll apprise them of inventions
They will work with in their minds
And bring them forth at certain times

And we think you would all agree
That at this time in history
The secret knowledge these stones hold
Must be made active by the bold
Who come to us from all directions
Standing in these bold erections
Called to visit wise ones, tall
And break the spell that they are small

Many of you have come before
Initiates old knew what's in store
As Earth now stands before the door
A perilous time that you are in
How great the ignorance and the sin
As shameless leaders create spin
That tricks the masses, sucks them in

You, good-hearted ones who weep
For all the folk who are asleep
You are a living bridge of grace
We look with pride upon your face

Find a circle, sacred place
That when you see it makes heart race
Worry not if you can't get there
We are here to make you aware

The metaphor of circles, divine
Concerns the power of your mind
Whose faculties were overtaken
By outside interests, those forsaken
Ones who think they run this place
Well, we are here to change the pace

Now let's get back to your great minds
That hold a hidden wand, divine
The time is now to learn to use
This wand within that they've abused
Your thinking habits must be changed
Your neural networks rearranged

It's time to call the knowledge back and access secrets, old
This is a task that you can hack, rise to the moment, bold
In the center of your chest there sits a cauldron, hot
Technology once placed in you, that you have not been taught
Quite how to use effectively
And even, we'd say, magically
Combined with mind that has been cleared
And then effectively it's steered

The correct weaving of these tools
Creates a kind of inner battery
In this way you're no longer fools
And prey to the false flattery
Of what the constructs of your day persuade you all to be
Instead, you'll find your own design that sets your good soul free

This wondrous treasure you contain turns on your DNA

And in a kind of 'fast forward' your ignorance you'll slay
The body vessel that you're in is really like a ship
It has for long been programmed one way, we're about to flip
That program on its head and activate the codes within
But you must be on board for this in order that you win
The prize of gold, the knowledge old, of which you will remember
Is found within that great cauldron, beneath which burn the embers
That cast the light you hold within, running that great ship you steer
But that great light's become quite dim, your enemy is fear

We seek to cast a spell here now through this delivered rhyme
We say to those who've waited long that you are in the time
Of cosmic forces opening
And Shining Ones with their great wings
Will call you from your slumbering
To clear your mind of misperceptions
We will point to the direction
You must look for the inception
Bringing you a point of view
That you will recognize as true

The cauldron stoked by your heart's light
Magician's pyre you must ignite
Feel in your heart center palpably
The presence of something you cannot see
But rather feel it presently
And magnify it expertly

Be aware of this cauldron throughout the day
That provides the medium for the Fae
To undermine the spells of deception
We offer you a vast injection
Enabling you to feel the might
Of the beauty you hold, your true birthright

Combine the feel of cauldron in heart

With the power of mind that helps you start
Creating in ways that summon light
Casting out the dark of night
For in your mind there lies the Grail
Whose powers it is time to hail

Let go the stories you've outgrown
That keep you chained to a false home
Whatever you have thought to date
It's time for you to clear the slate
And still yourself to feel the beat
Stoked by that magic cauldron's heat

Create a vision in your mind
Call back to you ancestors, kind
Who'll help you fuel that ship you're in
Who'll give you knowledge to begin
To steer yourselves to waters, calm
Where you'll become the healing balm
That soothes the troubled among your folk
And by example you will stoke
Their fire within so they can see
That within them lives the mystery
This place within will set you free
It is with inner eyes you'll see

The veils are parting wide now, dears
We're in the time prophesied by seers
When communication will exceed
What imagination can conceive
And you will know yourselves again
Earth's people will once more be sane
And so know this to be your truth
Seek out our wisdom like a sleuth
We're found within that cauldron, bright
We're here to help you end this night...

Ancestral Kin

I feel a soft light pressed in close
Insisting that I hereby know
That I am flanked by kindreds, wise
They're here to help me realize
That this has been my mind's creation
This radio must change the station

This, one must be ready for
For most don't even know this door
Even exists, yet it remains
Accessible on earthly plane

This door can take lifetimes to find
So hidden is it in the mind
For everything is metaphor
The Holy Grail a symbol for
A deep held secret portal door

It takes wings to find this door
A birds-eye view to see the floor
And the skies above your head
Most don't see until they're dead

Dying while you're still awake
Man's limited offerings you'll forsake
You've called in winged ones of light
For restoration of your sight

We've placed among you many friends
On this sojourn they help you tend
To matters of a deeper nature
Their encouragement ensures
That you'll stay long enough to win
The treasure hidden deep within

This man you'll love is coming soon
His love will make your good heart swoon
You wonder if he'll come with death
As you inhale your final breath

That thought in mind's a metaphor
First cross the threshold of that door
This, a place where you can meet
Folk whose essence is most sweet

Now this door's found within the mind
Is it not said, you greet your kind
Through a meeting of the minds?
Cultivate that fertile soil
Inner garden's where you toil

You are in a unique season
Where Earth's people have lost reason
Bring your bounty to the table
Share your gifts now to enable
Others to see and to act
You must now engage with tact

They cast spells laid out for fools
In higher mind you hold the tools
Call to mind the winged one's view
That takes you out of sorcerer's stew

Rigorous practice happens now
Harness your thoughts and train them how
To rest in silent quietude
So you can supersede that mood
And open within the temple doors
That are found on higher floors

Nature helps you find this place
Through the beauty of her face
You're inspired deep within
It's there you'll find ancestral kin

Ancestors were worshipped by people of old
Who knew the power that they hold
Would help them as they walked life's path
They've come before, they know the math

Your bloodline traces back to we
The Shining Ones you call the Sidhe
Who sat with you beneath the trees
When once your good people could see

You've called us from the greenery
You've asked us, "Help my people see"
And so, like you, we've made a vow
That we'd return and teach you how
To call the magic back again
To this beleaguered earthly plane

And so, for you, steps carefully laid
Will lead away from this charade
Unto a place where sanity's found
Then potent wisdom you can ground

And with the minds of many folk
The ancient magic you'll invoke
The flames beneath that cauldron stoke
The brewing magic that will poke
A hole in bubbles that are false
We will ensure Earth finds her pulse...

For My Law Mentor

This friendship serves you like no other
This man who is like a brother
Has a mind that is designed
To see beyond the spell that binds

This good man's heart, though much abused
Serves well, a very different muse
Who leads him to libraries, grand
Where he has found the hidden hand
That conducts the orchestra
And puts forth a plethora
Of rules and regulations, stern
How his curious mind does burn
To search the deeper mysteries
And crack the codes of tyranny

This man teaches you very well
His actions herald the death knell
Of those who have for centuries
Cheated the ignorant with glee

His gamesmanship—the highest kind
This man, he thinks! Oh, how his mind
With curiosity does ponder
Of the muse, he is beyond her

With humor and diplomacy
This man teaches others to see
His efforts will bring just rewards
His knowledge they can ill afford
To cast aside for these are pearls
That possibly can change the world

So, listen, daughter wise, do know
Your friendship with this man will grow
Old friends through time who come together
Both enjoy a change of weather
And so, you share your expertise
And collaborate with ease
Tell him he is doing well
As he tends a growing swell
Of waking minds who walk the Earth
A fire in mankind he'll birth

This may sound quite grandiose
Yet we say, with the right dose
Of mental magic and good heart
A revolution you can start

We are here to set the course
And guide well, your great sails
Feel our hidden presence
We'll provide you with the rails
To grasp when ocean waves rise high
When storm clouds dominate the sky
For you have braved many a storm
Through lifetimes when you've assumed form

And many times you held great magic
In this life 'twill be no tragic
Episodes of grim demise
But rather you will realize
A very ancient kind of knowledge
One they don't teach in their college

This one's sought with diligence
It demands intelligence
It opens doors in psyche's halls
The more you seek, the louder it calls

For this is truth that's recognized
By those who hear and see with eyes
Unbound from dark spells with their curse
Both of you are here to nurse
The dawn that rises with its light
Each of you will guide through night
Those whose slumber has not passed
You will help them raise their mast
To defeat the scourge, profane
That has imprisoned this Earth plane

Take the lessons he's taught you
And educate the precious few
Who nod their heads, hearing your words
They do not think it's absurd
To question what their schools have taught
They're seeing that the system's fraught
With obvious greed and corruption
Teach them law for the induction
Of a mindset that will free
The many from their misery...

Message to Me

Daughter wise, stop worrying
Let we, the beings in you sing
You've opened door, so we bring rhyme
That we cast spells with every time

You've joined our nation of the bright
And we, with you, will end this night
For we bring ancient spells of light
The good kind, ones that end the plight
Of which you find you're in today
So, with our magic weave a way

Playing with those words you use
To help you fight those who abuse
We'll continue to imbue
Your heart with wisdom that is true

It's a kind of magic flute
You would think it's quite a hoot
For it disarms and opens hearts
Our magic will not tear apart

But rather weave its wisdom, old
Dear, wisdom reigns, put that in bold
Italics on your paper, white
Know daughter, that this long dark night
Is soon to end, the rain will bring
Change, and if you're wondering
Well dear, you're in the time of water
Pouring forth, assist that, daughter

Make it sweet, dear, use your honey
Bless it by making it funny
Win their hearts quite expertly
And with kindness you will weave
With we and many of like mind
The kind of world we'd like to find...

Winter Calls

It's time to rest in quiet slumber
Our leaves disappear in number
As one cycle closes door
Prepare to enter season four

Winter calls you to take note
Of how fast you move in rote
You, too, must slow down at times
Immerse yourself in peace, sublime

But sadly, man's forgotten all
Mankind ignores the daily call
To follow cycles, ancient old
Our folk once did what they were told

As they observed the natural world
They understood one would be hurled
Into a hell if they ignored
The ancient wisdom that was stored
In Nature's bounteous offerings
That when beheld made good hearts sing

The corporate spell now takes its toll
Enslaving planet Earth's their goal
In ignorance, man suffers and toils
In contract trickery, he's embroiled

Nature seeks to break the spell
Inside the mind is where it dwells
The corporate mindset is a trick
It's hoped you'll wake within the nick
Of time before you've lost it all
Because you've ignored Nature's call

And so, for winter's slower time
We ask you, ponder this short rhyme
Slow down your rushing to and fro
To rest and let your worries go

Sit outside beneath a tree
Let your harried mind be free
Let your body slowly breathe
Protective barriers unsheathed
Open your heart and let it swell
As we provide you with a well
Whose wisdom waters nourish you
And lead you into what is true

Nature's calls, you must now heed
She provides the food that feeds
Your bodies and your hearts and minds
This spell you're in she will unbind...

By the River with the Fae

The water flows here by and by
This gracious stream makes my heart fly
The birds so sweet here in the trees
Their song it does set my heart free

The sound of water rushing by
The kind that's easy on the eyes
Oh, how I love to stand today
And greet the spirits called the Fae

I feel you here upon this land
As I stand here, extended hand
Calling you, good spirits, wise
I ask you, help me open eyes
To this great power I behold
I feel myself held in the fold
Of your embrace so sweetly kind
Standing here, I feel my mind
Is soothed for now, my worries, past
And I can open heart at last

So many shades I see of green
So numerous I've never seen
The leaves beginning shifting hue
It's almost time to bid adieu
As fall begins its soft goodbye
And winter beckons by and by

Response from the Fae:

The changing seasons showing you
That like the mind we can construe
And so, dear, what we say is true
That winter comes to we and you

And though it may feel frightful cold
You must know now that this is old
And though your heart, it bears the burden
Of the suffering and the hurting
Know, dear, as you've wisely said
You cannot quiet the dead

The light, it lives through thick and thin
And in this game, dear, it will win
Of course it must, so trust us, here
We will make this very clear

Feel the wind caressing you
Yes, we know that you feel blue
But remember just as we
Seasons pass and then you're free

And so let fall do what it will
Let go your troubles, wait until
The winter comes to help you grow
This year may even see some snow
And then the spring will call you, dear
With new beginnings, do not fear

And for your ladies lying there
They, too, will become aware
That in them lives the faerie magic
They've the keys to lift the tragic
Spell of loss of memory
Those good women, they will see

As you scry upon the water
Watch the movement, lonely daughter
Watch the way the raindrops fall
Take it in, dear, watch it all

It forms for you the information
Understood within your nation
Watch transfixed and we will show
The water it does swiftly flow

At every corner many changes
As the water rearranges
Know that we won't give the answer
Though you know this Earth has cancer

We can't tell you 'twill be healed
Doesn't matter if you kneel
We no more have that answer, dear
Than those great monsters that you fear

We simply know that things must flow
And one season must end and go
And then another comes to be
And like you, we will wish it free

We stand and rise and greet the Sun
And greet the Moon and everyone
From birds to the four-legged ones
And so, good daughter, it's not done
For many are arising here
As situations become clear

That, dear one, will help to steer
The climate that is run on fear
Into a place of clarity
Where more and more begin to see
The beauty of what could be lost
Of what could be a long-lived frost

And so bright poet standing there
We feel, we sense you clearly care

Drink deeply of this forest nation
And then share the situation

We'll just say that you might be
That you might be quite pleasantly
Surprised to know that we have friends in awfully high positions
And the powers that be here and now, they might just be a-switchin'
That's our little ear-to-ear
As we whisper so you'll hear

And so dear poet, take this beauty
Hold it close, that is your duty
As you see the gray clouds change
Know blue skies will rearrange

So many forces active now
You cannot imagine how
But winds of change, dear, have a way
Of surprising even *they*

Trust in us, the ancient ones
You, good daughter of the Sun
For this new age, it has begun
And shine we will
We're far from done...

Invitation from the Trees

Come and we will teach you more
We are just outside your door
Visit more often, daughter dear
Always know that we are near

Watching you with great affection
We'll give you a green injection
Opening that heart of yours
Ready for that wondrous door?

We ask you, dear, what doors are made of...
See dear one, dear earthly native?
Now you know, you see our gift
And your good heart will surely lift

Cleave to us so you can hear
The ones who stand so tall and near
The wisdom folk here in your yard
We want to help you though it's hard
For you to hear, you get so busy
Watching you it makes us dizzy
Always in a kind of tizzy
Yet we wait while you stay busy

Come to us and share your heart
And to you, dear one, we'll impart
Stories old and wisdom, true
All of that belongs to you...

Cauldron Song

Bring back now the cauldron mysteries
That have disappeared from history
This, an ancient alchemy
Given so initiates see

Penetrate the sacred bowl
Hold it fast within your soul
Within the cauldron waters churn
The embers below they do burn

Tended by nine cosmic maidens
Powers here will not be fadin'
Creation's kitchen, this the place
The cauldron you must all now face

Its waters of wisdom and of knowledge
Gift you with an ancient college
Its curriculum is vast
It will raise your vessel's mast

The elements you'll understand
The great wind will extend its hand
You'll brave the storms with courage, fine
Your vessel light, 'twill be divine

The Sun will then pour forth its rays
The sound of birdsong sweetly plays
A melody you'll understand
For Nature is the greatest band
This concert books up very fast
For no one knows how long it lasts
And so, you come for harmony
And lend your unique melody
In hopes the music will be sweet
To dance here truly is a treat

And so, we'll play with musical words
Using the metaphor of the birds
Whose morning song lifts spirits high
And tells you that the day is nigh

Their harmony delights the soul
And so, they're found in cauldron's bowl
This musical chamber you are in
Nature's sounds, how sweet the din

When mankind is in harmony
The Earth, it sings with heartfelt glee
But when mankind forgets the tune
The notes fall flat and very soon
The harmony, sick and contorted
Causes life to be distorted

Sound is simply frequency
A vibration that you can't see
How you think and how you speak
How you act and what you seek
All are quite like musical notes
Sung by souls who sail in boats
Great vessels you sail in the seas
As you explore life's mysteries

Please mind the choreography
As you explore geography
Put forth a tune of high vibration
That lifts the people of your nation
Then invite in Nature's songs
She always likes to sing along...

Rays Through Morning Mist

Effulgent morning rays shine bright
They pierce the mist left from the night
What a greeting from my door
Dusty rays I stand before

The rays through trees form morning star
That calls me to this magic hour
I feel the cauldron in my heart
Respond in kind as every part
Of body mind and spirit, here
Join in with Nature's morning cheer

Most are too busy to behold
This misty magic in the cold
Of early morning's quiet song
Inviting us to sing along

Lift your head up from your screen
Behold the magic that is seen
As Nature kindly welcomes you
To greet the morn and birth anew

Another day you walk this Earth
Another chance for you to birth
Your own heart's light that pierces mist
Bathed in that light you'll get the gist

Of how to touch the hand of Nature
Reaching out to her you ensure
Your ability to calm
She provides you with the balm

That stabilizes busy mind
Inspiring you with a kind

Of beauty quickening up the soul
Inviting you to become whole

Hand extended through the trees
Sunlight's rays like shimmering bees
Hum and dance in morning's mist
Spend time in Nature, she insists

Nature's beauty breaks the spell
Her offerings will make you well
So take some time from the rat race
To feel a very different pace

Time spent in Nature's embrace
Will bring a smile unto your face
More effective than those pills
That ultimately make you ill

For Nature's gifts to you are free
So watch as sunlight pierces tree
Her morning rays inspiring you
To cast your light, for when you do
It's felt by many around you
Compelling others to construe
A better way to see things through
And so, the morning beckons you
To drink the nectar of her dew...

Word Spells

Let's investigate how spells
Are cast to either make you well
Or trip you up to make life hell

This concerns the depth of mind
Coupled with words a spell does bind
For sound is a wand whose power is such
That whoever can hear can be easily clutched

Then there's the ancient magic of words
That can sing and captivate like birds
Words enchant the mind and heart
They initiate the start
Of a response within you of some kind
Next thing you know, you're in a bind
Of sorts, that holds that place
Whether you're glued to page's face
Or compelling conversation
The power of words has gripped your nation

You respond accordingly
The spell is cast and you don't see
How you've been captured easily

The conjured subject, you think is real
You're captivated by the spiel
That initiates a cascade of response
A spell now cast and you're ensconced

You participate in the weave
A tapestry is then conceived
And if you don't like the design
You must reweave it in your mind
Now you are doing mental knitting
How inconvenient and yet fitting

You think you are no artisan
But when caught in bipartisan
Engagement you're caught in the art
Of spelling with words, you play your part

And so, let's do this consciously
Consider the power of words to weave
Consider the sound of their vibration
Of how they affect corresponding nations

You can cast spells on yourself
That art long taught by Fae and Elf
Who've observed mankind for a long time
And know full well the power of rhyme

A different form of interplay
Bringing a new spin to the day
Note that there is many a spell
Conjured with rhyme to direct it well
This, a novel way to use
Those pesky words that get abused

So, we invite you now to play
When your good mood falls away
Interrupt that same old fray
Compose a rhyme that shifts the day

Imagine you've got Elf and Fae
Nearby to coach you all the way
We'll put a smile upon your face
We will help you to erase
The wicked spells that infect you
And cause your thoughts to direct to
The negative patterns that keep you
From accessing the treasure that's found
In higher mind, the fertile ground

Where creative intuition lives
A generous place that loves to give
A treasure trove of ideas, bright
That rescues you from dark of night

And so, play now with rhymes that weave
A new reality you'll conceive
A simple shift of words that play
That turn dark night into the day

Know that this way of weaving words
Changes vibrations that are heard
And felt by many others near
Who, if they could, would give a cheer
To hear once more poetic sounds
That lift good hearts up from the ground
Initiating ancient magic
Through a clever vocal gadget
Your good voice to use with care
To cast your spells that fill the air...

Stay the Course

Ireland calls you to the hour
This, another place of power
Have faith like initiates, old
Who faced the unknown with a bold
Sense of purpose and of knowing
Daughter, we will say, you're growing

Far more tuned in, as you say
Calling magic to the day
Take your mind to clarity, sure
Use the cauldron in heart, pure

This a habit you create
It will take you to a state
Of standing in the grace of knowing
That is when those seeds you're sowing
Will take root, then bud and flower
You will reach that hoped-for hour

This, the practice we give you
We'll give more examples, too
And you will face each one as tall
Initiates do not play small

Put your words upon the page
You are in creation's stage
Where ideas must come forth
You're inspired by the north
Place of ancestral abiding
It is with you we are siding

Feel us flanking you right now
Ask us and we'll show you how
To walk through chaos unafraid

It is we pipers you have paid
Attention to for several years
We are mentors for the seers

Play your own pipe now, good daughter
Play the notes of wisdom's waters
Sing through flute and pages white
Sing your ancient song of light
Sing your inspiration, sweet
You are getting to the meat
Of this great mystery you are in
Let that sink beneath your skin

You can see while others can't
Bring the wisdom where it's scant
Write and speak and play your tune
And we will join in very soon...

Conjuring

You're in the place of conjuring
This a time when souls can sing
The spells will break before your eyes
For some 'twill come as a surprise

While others who have watched with care
Who see spellcasting everywhere
Will start to conjure their own spells
Designed to make this planet well

These spells do not imprison minds
These spells are of a different kind
The seer's eye is quite the find
Though others prefer to stay blind

Look to the stars as once was done
The planets that share with the Sun
The universe, that cosmic clock
Has long been used to tame the flock
Magnetics that affect the Earth
Work with that and you will birth
Some very pleasant happenings
Those magnetics lend their wings

Assisting you in conjuring
The visions that you wish to spring
Forth to a world caught up in woe
This, the time to call out, NO!

Explore in mind the untapped treasure
So much power, you can't measure
Clear the spells that bind your thoughts
This takes work, you must allot
Certain moments day and night
To develop inner sight

These inner actions are a way
To exercise your power
Taking time throughout the day
This discipline will shower
You with many resources
That you can call to bear
Rather than be led by fools
You'll choose a different stair

See the potent spells you blast
Then you will learn very fast
How easily the web is cast
Thoughts, then words, they set the pace
Actions follow, then the face
Of your reality abides
This play you're in fares well or slides

Train your mind, these spells to see
Activate your clarity
Study just how easily
The average personality
Gets caught up in passion play
That sticky web affects the day

Conjuring will not go well
Until you see the many spells
When you see how they set the stage
How easily they turn the page
Your mind will wake, you'll have a choice
To activate a different voice
That lives within you, deeply held
It is a wisdom you can meld
Into this passion play of life
Wise words and actions can slay strife

In this way you'll conjure well
This, the starting point to dwell
Upon to notice everyday
How you participate in ways
That either serve to clear the fray
Or make a mess that keeps the haze
Of ignorance upon this place
So practice well, this is the ace
You're given now to change the pace...

Reminder

We are still here daughter, bright
We stand by you day and night
You think that the signal's dim
Take that busy mind and trim
Those crowded thoughts that shout and play
And keep you in that nonstop fray

All those binding spells in there
Seek to keep you unaware
Do you see how thoughts in mind
Contract your soul and deftly bind
You to a way of always being
That gets in the way of seeing?

This is elementary
The basics, rudimentary
In the mind is where you start
To cast the magic to impart
The spell, whose frequency is light
That wakes the sleeping from their night
Of deep sound slumber, unaware
Of magic they are holding there

A pot of gold in rainbow's care
Is ready now for all to share
Though some see only rainbow's hue
They see surface but not through

Think of it as a kind of veil
Appearing after storm or gale
It calls out in a different way
It breaks the spell with its display

You see it and you're stirred somehow
Its beauty has caused horse and plow
To simply pause and still the mind
And for a moment it unwinds
To receive Nature's beauty call
A message sent to one and all

Activate us in your heart
Feel the magic we impart
Simply pause a moment there
To see Nature everywhere

Even when in crowded city
You can find an itty-bitty
Piece of Nature that will charm
Like a gentle clock's alarm
To rouse you from unconscious thoughts
That when unchecked become a clot
And that is when you just cannot
Connect to teachers who have taught
In your waking and your dreams
Though at times to you it seems
That you just walk this path alone
And our connection's turned to stone
Yet we beckon, come outside
And Nature's frequencies you'll ride

We call you in many ways
Trying hard to shift that daze
You are in from those diversions
Each one is a deep immersion
Yes, it can be hard to hear
The unseen ones who stand so near

Use these teachings on the mind
So you'll see and not be blind

Look for Nature's avenue
It's the road we call you to

We put forth our own excursions
Calling you from those diversions
To a place that's truly real
Offering clarity you can feel

A place where you can gather thoughts
The ones that deftly untie knots
This, the place of inspiration
That you feel within your nation

Sages old have found us here
Seeking ways that they can clear
Their minds and then the minds of others
They'd share wisdom with their brothers

See your good mind like a garden
Tend the soil, don't let it harden
As well, don't let those thoughts like weeds
Take root and choke out the good seeds

We provide enlivening power
To what you plant and tend each hour
There is more we will teach you
For today just learn these few
Suggestions we want you to master
Steering you from that disaster
Of a play that's run its course
Seducing all away from Source...

The Guardians

Feel the guardians here now
Flanking you, we'll teach you how
We present another layer
To the answer to your prayer
This is co-creative, dear
You've called us and we are here

We now help you lift the veil
Behind which lies the Holy Grail
Held in mind it quietly waits
Until you're ready to open the gate

Feel the warmth of cauldron in heart
Clear your mind so you can part
The waves of misperceptions, great
To do this you must clear the slate

Then feel the Shining Ones here now
These three steps will teach you how
To walk as one who knows she hails
From distant star beyond the gales

Your kindreds call you to the hour
This, the time to summon power
You will shatter fantasy
And with clear mind begin to see
What you think of as revelation
It will change you in your nation

The mind is an exquisite tool
Woefully misused by fools
You must train to take it back
For at this time your thoughts attack
They make a mess and create flack

Be disciplined and do not slack
The clearer the mind
The easier to bind
With higher spells that free your kind

Our voices louder as you repeat
The essence of them is most sweet
For you have called in mentors, wise
Who will ensure you'll realize
The lessons you came here to learn
Will stoke the fire there that burns
Beneath the cauldron in heart center
We're preparing you to enter
Into what's an ancient grove
Within that circle you once strove
To be an adept who had knowledge
One who walked as living college

In this grove you spoke to stars
Who called you there at certain hours
During those times you sat with kin
Shining Ones you welcomed in
Though time's passed and your form's new
Do not dare think we'd forget you
We will ensure you will remember
The sorcerer's spell we will dismember
Practice daily these three ways
Collect yourself over the days
This will clear the mental haze
And take you to a higher phase...

Mushroom Faerie illustration from *The Peacock and the Wishing-Fairy*,
Corrine Ingraham, 1921.

Conjuring a Cottage

*Until one is committed, there is hesitancy, the chance to draw back,
always ineffectiveness. Concerning all acts of initiative (and creation),
there is one elementary truth—the ignorance of which kills countless
ideas and splendid plans: that the moment one definitely commits
oneself, then providence moves too. A whole stream of events issues from
the decision, raising in one's favor all manner of unforeseen incidents,
meetings and material assistance, which no man could have dreamt
would have come his way. I learned a deep respect for one of Goethe's
couplets: "Whatever you can do or dream you can, begin it. Boldness
has genius, power and magic in it!"*

– W. H. Murray

In 2016 I received a psychic message that when my younger daughter
graduated in 2019, I was to leave the Pacific Northwest for good and move
"east coast, rural." I was not given the exact place but I began to think
about where I wanted to move after leaving my cottage on a horse farm in
Redmond, Washington. I conjured the Redmond cottage with focus and
dedication and it came to me very serendipitously. My next abode came
in such a wildly magical way that most people simply wouldn't believe it,
but I assure you, what I'm sharing is accurate and true.

I decided that what I wanted was a nineteenth century farmhouse
on a minimum of three acres with a barn in the back, for sale by owner,
for under two-hundred thousand dollars, within an hour of the airport
and perfect for my retreats. At that time, I had no money saved, as I'd
just started doing retreats and I wasn't charging much for them initially.

I will first give a quick account of how my retreats got started. I had
been working with the mushroom for about four years and at the age of
fifty-two I was teaching shamanic practices and doing Skype sessions for
psycho-spiritual counseling. I had been working with a lovely woman in
the Michigan area when she asked if it would be at all possible to fly out
and stay with me for a few days and soak up some of my knowledge, and
have me sit for her on a mushroom journey. I told her I'd think about it,

as it had never occurred to me to work with people in that way and I had to figure out where that would even take place. My dear friend offered me the use of his home in the Washington rainforest, so I made arrangements with my client, and a few weeks later she flew to Seattle where I picked her up and made the three-hour drive to his place. We spent three powerful days together in that gorgeous part of the world and I joined her on the mushroom journey, which I spoke of in the chapter, Messages from the Forest Folk.

The following week I had a client who would come for her weekly session in person and I casually told her about my experience the prior week. She got excited and, pulling out her checkbook from her purse she asked, "You do that? How much do you charge?" I was not expecting that at all but needless to say, I found myself on another road-trip to the rainforest with another lovely woman, and that retreat was also just wonderful. Upon my return, my law mentor asked if I would consider working with a couple, as he'd told his friends in New Jersey what I was doing and they wanted to fly out and work with me. That too, went very well and I started to realize this was going to continue.

I then began to map out a structure and timeframe along with cost and then added the retreat offering discreetly to my website. Suffice to say that I am now in my ninth year of hosting one-on-one retreats and have worked with over three-hundred people, men and women from the ages of eighteen to eight-four. There were a few years there where I hosted retreats back-to-back almost every week of the year, which sounds insane but I dearly loved the work and I have been blessed with a lot of energy and stamina. I have savored the privilege of witnessing another's mystery and holding space for their unfolding, and I have been dearly blessed to have attracted the most beautiful people to me, some of whom would return annually and a few who have become dear friends. The retreats have been my heart's work and I've basically lived like a nun these past several years, cocooned in my sweet cottage space, serving the Sacred in my own unique way. I am at the end of that chapter as I write this book and moving forward, I will be focusing more on teaching, mentoring, and writing.

Back to 2016, I was given the news of a whole new chapter beginning in just three years that would include the purchase of a home. It may sound hard to believe to some but having struggled through my life with chronic worry and at times crippling self-doubt, I never thought I would be able to make a good living on my own, much less buy a house. I'm long past that limited way of thinking now thanks to the mushroom teachers and diligent work on myself. One of the very important lessons my mushroom teachers stressed for me was to learn to trust and to relax into the process as new experiences were forming.

I began to think about where on the east coast I would want to live. One of the women I met in Scotland lived in Nova Scotia, so in January of 2017 I flew out for a visit to see if that might be a possibility. I was born in Canada and have lived in the US for over forty years. I'd never been to Nova Scotia and after spending a few days there I was smitten with the rocky beauty of its coastline, the charm of the area, particularly Mahone Bay, and the warmth of the people. During my stay, I sat for my host who ate mushrooms for the first time. I ate a few myself and while she was deep in her journey, I received the following message:

Keep alive that lovely dream
Though at times it may well seem
Like an uphill climb for you
We say your money woes are through
You must be clear and focus well
Use your mind to cast the spell
Call to you that lovely place
See it right before your face
See yourself upon that land
We will all give you a hand
With emotion beckon that
We, all of us, will tip our hat
You, a daughter of the north
This snowy island calls you forth
This place of beauty, blue/green grace
How nicely it does slow the pace

> So much magic it does hold
> Beckoning you, daughter bold...

I remember reading it the following day and noting the line, "This snowy island calls you forth," and thinking that Nova Scotia isn't an island, it's a peninsula. I know that the Sidhe play with words and that the words that come forth aren't by accident so that detail stayed with me. Before I left Nova Scotia, I was invited by a friend of my host to house-sit for her in the summer for two weeks. That would give me ample time to immerse myself in the area and decide if it was indeed the place for me. I returned home with the dream in my head of moving to that rustically beautiful place and continued to work with retreat clients as they came in. That summer I flew back and during my stay I found an old house for sale on a hill in a rather remote area with a view of the ocean. The entire house would need to be gutted and though I love renovation and design I did not yet have enough saved for a down payment, much less a major renovation. A few months after returning home and much thought on the idea of leaving the US, I realized that Nova Scotia was not the right choice for me.

I will say that from the time I knew what I wanted for myself I said frequently out loud, "I want a nineteenth century cottage with a barn in the back on three acres, for sale by owner, for under two-hundred thousand, within an hour from the airport, and perfect for my retreats." In conversation I would say that I was going to be buying a farmhouse in the northeast. I had no clue how that was going to happen or how the money would come to make such a purchase, but I repeated that statement often, as repetition builds the charge of the intention. I knew what I had been told, that in 2019 I was to move to the east coast, rural. By then, I trusted in the Sidhe. They are playful but they are not deceitful. They enjoy giving me clues and riddles and I am expected to do the digging and this was no different. I had apprenticed myself to the mushroom teachers and as apprentice, part of my schooling was to get my mind right to where I could set it like a dial to a specific goal and then summon the vision, focus and will to see it through. Vision. Focus. Will. That is my formula for conjuring, along with my magical alliance with this exquisite race of beings who do not coddle me, by the way, nor do they grant wishes like some silly Disney character. I co-create with them and as I am in an earthly body this go-around, I have to do the footwork to cultivate the charge or spell using the power of my mind, my imagination and my will.

Almost daily I would picture in my mind that I was on a path and I could see my cottage up ahead. I wasn't watching myself walking the path, I *was* walking the path. Along the path, halfway submerged in the ground were smooth river rocks that represented my doubts and fears and undermining voices. As they were half buried, they were muffled and I walked steadily on, ignoring them and focusing all my attention on what I envisioned my house to be. I saw that it was painted white with a front porch and I would walk up the steps to the porch and put my key in the door. It would open wide to a gorgeous kitchen and living area and my heart would just swoon. I would feel the full emotion of knowing this was my precious treasure and I was finally home. I would walk through the house and I would feel a visceral sensation in my body of sheer happiness and gratitude. The more often I did this the stronger the image was in my mind and the surer I was that it would happen. That is called building a charge field and the greater field will respond in time.

At the start of 2018 I began receiving poetic messages about my future home in rapid-fire succession every month until it materialized later that year. The poetry was a huge assist for my mind-state, as the words were comforting and encouraging and I followed their advice in earnest. I knew I wanted to be in the northeast and I had to find an area that was affordable, as I couldn't afford an expensive house in the first place and I did not want to be house-poor. Also, my work was on the downlow and I knew that no bank would give me a mortgage, which was why I knew I had to work out a private deal in a for-sale-by-owner situation. I had always loved Maine and in early spring of 2018 I flew to Portland where I stayed with one of the other women I had met in Scotland, and the third woman I'd met there was also in Maine, which made it a very attractive possibility. We drove to a number of towns on my visit and even looked at a few homes for sale but I knew as soon as I got off the plane that Maine wasn't a 'yes'. It wasn't a 'no' but I wasn't getting a 'yes', and we all know what a 'yes' feels like.

Back home I thought of New Hampshire or possibly Vermont and in early summer one of my retreat clients flew me to Vermont to do more medicine work with her at her weekend cottage. It was near Middlebury and we explored that charming historic town and the surrounding area. I had recently returned from co-leading a small tour in Ireland and I commented that it had the feel of Ireland but with more trees. I was very taken by the beauty of Vermont and I loved the New England-style architecture, the farmland, the painted red barns, the cows... This was my place!

After that I regularly scoured Zillow, looking for the perfect house with the perfect price, for sale by owner. In early August I flew to California to teach and before boarding the flight home I found a new listing on Zillow. It was for a Victorian cottage with an old red barn in the back on Isle La Motte, which I learned is the northernmost island on Lake Champlain. Who knew there were islands in Vermont? It was on almost three acres, for sale by owner with an asking price of $179,500, and it was exactly an hour from Burlington Airport.

I sent the listing to my friend who'd flown me to Vermont earlier that summer and I just happened to be flying to New York in two days for a visit. She emailed me back and suggested we drive up there to check the place out. Right away I got the feeling that this was being choreographed somehow by my shining friends. It was just too perfect. How it would all come together was another matter but something told me it was out of my hands and I was not to worry but rather pay attention to the signs and hold the vision.

The following day I called the seller and we hit it off immediately. He was a schoolteacher and a very nice man. He and his wife had purchased the house a few years before and did some much-needed renovation and lived there for a while but quickly outgrew it. They rented it to another schoolteacher who had just moved out and they chose to sell it without using a realtor. I was very candid from the get-go, saying that I'd been searching for this exact house for the past couple of years, that I could only do it as a for sale by owner, and that it was perfect for the retreat work I did. He said there was interest in it from people who were thinking of it as a summer home when I blurted out, "I'm looking at it as my forever home and I'm going to call it, Faerie-Tree Cottage." Now, my daughters would absolutely die of embarrassment if they heard me say such a thing and I can't believe I said that, but his response was even more shocking. He replied, "That's funny, my wife and I were just at a Faerie festival earlier this summer!"

There are moments when you realize life is not at all what we've been led to believe. There are moments when you realize you are not in Kansas anymore.

This was definitely one of those moments.

My response to that was to go full disclosure and share that my work involved magic mushrooms and that I channel the Sidhe. I figured, by then we were done with any kind of formalities and were on a completely different wavelength of understanding, and indeed we were. I told him I'd be flying to New York in a couple of days and asked if I could look at the house and he said he'd leave the key and to take all the time I needed.

Three days later my friend and I made the 6-hour drive from New York City to Isle La Motte and arrived in darkness. We were looking for our bed and breakfast when I happened to look out the window just as we were passing my house! I was bursting with excitement and anticipation and we soon found our way to our sweet bed and breakfast overlooking Lake Champlain. It had a screened-in front porch and after we got settled, I went downstairs and stood in the porch looking out onto the moonlit lake as a gust of summer wind blew toward me, flooding me with memories of summers at the cottage as a child in Ontario.

Isle La Motte is seven miles long and two miles wide with a yearlong population of just over five hundred people, ballooning to almost two thousand in the summer when the Quebecoise cross the Canadian border just twenty minutes away to enjoy the beauty of northern Vermont. On Isle La Motte there happens to be a shrine to Mother Mary's mother, Saint Anne. As a child, Mother Mary was the only element to church that I felt a kinship with and that stayed with me through my adulthood. At the shrine there is a huge copper statue gilded in gold of Mother Mary on a tall octagonal base with a halo of stars above her head and golden roses at her feet. That was not lost on me, as I thought it quite the coincidence that I would find myself on an 'isle' with a shrine to the divine mother. And let's not forget the message I received on the mushroom while in Nova Scotia, and my perplexity on their choice of the word, 'island' rather than 'peninsula'. That line, *"this snowy island calls you forth."* Well, Isle La Motte, being an island by the Canadian border and all, gets its fair share of snow. So, there's that.

The next day, we visited the house and I fell in love with it as I knew I would. It was situated in the historic part of tiny Isle la Motte, surrounded by the most beautiful mature maple trees. In fact, I was struck by the grandeur of the trees and so many of them were huge old specimens. I had my measuring tape with me and began drawing floorplans of each room as I had learned over twenty years prior when I attended Parson's School of Design. There was a lot more renovation I wanted to do on that house but first of course, I had to figure out how I was going to buy it.

I had twenty thousand dollars saved by then and if I had surrounded myself with naysayers, which I didn't, of course, they would have said something to the effect of, "That's unrealistic, no bank is going to give you a mortgage and neither is someone selling their house. There's no way you'll have enough money to make that kind of purchase, etc. etc." Well, fortunately, I was listening to my inner teachers and this lifelong worrier and doubter was learning to trust no matter what.

I returned home on Sunday and on Monday I worked with a retreat client for the rest of the week. She was a bright sensitive woman and I shared with her my story of the house I'd just seen. I had a phone meeting with the sellers the following Saturday and she wished me luck as I dropped her at the airport. When I spoke with the sellers, they told me they wanted me to have the house but they explained that in order for me to pay them directly instead of a bank, they would need to pay off the balance of their mortgage so they could hold the note and I would make monthly payments to them. I asked them how much was left on the mortgage and they said ninety-five thousand dollars. I had twenty thousand. I needed another seventy-five thousand yesterday.

On Monday morning I received a text from the prior week's retreat client that absolutely blew my mind and broke open my heart. She wrote, "I know you're going to say no but I want to support your work. I want to lend you twenty-thousand toward that house." I felt my eyes fill with tears and I texted her back to accept and discuss how to structure the loan. I couldn't believe what just happened.

Two days after my phone call with the sellers I was now up to forty thousand dollars.

A day later I got a call from my dear friend in the Washington Rainforest who said, "I don't want you to leave but I'll loan you twenty-thousand toward that house." I about fell off my chair. I had no idea he had that kind of money available, much less to loan out, and I was deeply moved by his generosity and kindness. I was in a state of both excitement and disbelief at how this was coming together. I was now up to sixty-thousand toward my dream. I wondered how I was going to possibly gather the rest of the money.

The following day I received a text from my birth father and before I go on, I will give you the backstory. I was adopted at around four months old. My birth-mother tried keeping me for a few months but it just didn't work out. I was very fortunate to be adopted by very nice people who I call my parents. My father who adopted me died when I turned fifty and my mother is still alive and well. I always wondered about my birth parents and in my early twenties I contacted the Adoption Disclosure Agency in Toronto. The deal was I had to send in a request form and if my birth-mother or birth-father had done the same, there would be a match and we could meet. If not, I would just have to wait. Well, a couple of months before that, my birth mother at the suggestion of her daughter, contacted the agency and sent in her request. To both our astonishment, a match was made and we met soon thereafter.

She had kept in touch with my birth-father and contacted him with the news. Soon after, I met him in New York where I was living and later met his grown children, my half-brother and two half-sisters. Unfortunately, my birth-father's wife didn't want him to be in touch with me for various reasons and in order to keep the peace, he did what he felt was right, though I did talk with him a few times over the years and I met his mother, my nana. There is a sweet story there to share as well.

As an infant, my birth mother used to drop me at my nana and grandpa's house and disappear for a week or more. It was my nana's desire to raise me but she had her hands full and eventually it was an attorney friend of hers who arranged my adoption through the Catholic Children's Aid. Of course, this man couldn't tell my nana who adopted me but he did tell her it was a couple from her parish, Saint Edwards Church. Well, every Sunday for the next few years my nana would go to church and scour the pews in the hope of catching a glimpse of me. It never happened but she never stopped thinking of and praying for me. I was able to visit her in Toronto after meeting my birth father and it was a very special experience.

Well, at the age of forty-nine, my father who adopted me passed away from cancer. It was a great loss and then a year later, out of the blue I got a phone call from my birth-father. He told me his wife had recently passed and he very much wanted to know his daughter and his granddaughters. It was extraordinary timing and I realized I had lost a father and then gained a father, and we have been close ever since and I love him dearly.

That brings me back to the text I received from him that fated week. His text said that he wanted to give me twenty-thousand dollars. I was beside myself. How could this be happening? I already had a father who raised me and this good man on the other side of that text owed me nothing yet here was his offer. When we spoke, I told him I had arrangements with two other people who were lending me money and I would work out something similar with him, to which he answered that he wasn't lending me anything. He informed me he had put me in his will, and this money was an advance to be used for the purchase of my house. Words cannot convey the emotion I felt when he told me that. It was an overwhelming feeling of being deeply moved and struggling to accept such an authentically loving gesture.

And by the way, not one of these generous souls is wealthy. They are hard-working, solid people who genuinely wanted to help me and I am ever-blessed to this day by their good grace.

Well, now I was up to eighty-thousand dollars and I texted the sellers to ask if they would be open to ponying up the last fifteen thousand

and we could make the deal happen. The seller texted me back to say they'd just received a flurry of offers and he would get back to me. I had a moment there as you can imagine. However, I knew something that those bidders didn't. Because I had such a candid connection with the seller, he'd told me they had spent so much money on the renovation that they were actually selling the house at a loss, which meant bidding lower, which is what most people do, would not get them that house.

I texted him back to say I was not a wealthy woman and was not in a position to get into any kind of bidding war, but I would pay $3500 above asking and do a loan with them at 5%. He texted back to say he'd get back to me. Well, two days later I hadn't heard anything and my birth-father called to see what was up. When I told him he said, "We can't let this get away from us! I'll give you the other fifteen thousand."

This generous, honorable man who was not in a position to marry my birth-mother and raise me all those years ago, now stepped up to the plate for me in a way that I will be ever grateful for, not only because he made that house happen for me, but he stepped up to the plate from a place of pure fatherly love. I never blamed him for what happened to me as a baby or for having to step back at the behest of his wife after we finally got to meet. It just never occurred to me to have any kind of bad feeling about that because life is complicated and things happen and people make decisions out of necessity and hopefully with the best intentions. But that moment was a deep and unexpected healing for me where I felt loved in a very profound way that a very tiny infant part of me was craving and in that moment that tiny infant was soothed and blessed and put to rest peacefully.

I picked up the phone and called the sellers and said "I've got your mortgage payoff funds. Let's make this happen."

After the closing in early October, I knew I needed to find a good contractor to do the extensive renovation that needed to happen before I moved there in June of 2019. I figured I was on a roll with my manifesting so I asked the Sidhe to please bring to me an honest contractor who is darn good at his job, reasonably priced, older and experienced and local to the island. I called the sellers and asked who they could recommend and they gave me the name of their contractor. They told me he does excellent work and is very reasonable and he grew up on the island. Mission accomplished.

I made the call and introduced myself and discussed the project with him. We had an easy rapport and I knew this was a good man. At one point he asked, "Will you be flying out here to do a walk-through?" I said, "Nope." He said, "So you're just going to trust me?" And I said, "Yup." He told me a couple of years later that he still tells people that story.

My retreats at that time were fully booked and I worked every week till Christmas that year with bookings into 2019. In late December I took a deep breath and sent my contractor a starting check for twenty-five thousand dollars. I was not taking out any loans, I planned to pay for this with my own money. He and his brothers began the work in January of 2019 and I had to trust that I would have the money to complete the work that consisted of gutting the two bedrooms upstairs, replacing the stairway, redoing the kitchen, putting in wood flooring and much more. No one who would have purchased that house would have spent the money I spent but that house was almost two hundred years old and I wanted to do right by that old beauty and so it was. That said, I had butterflies in my tummy at times in early 2019, concerned that I might not make enough to finish the job. I received two very encouraging transmissions at that time that helped me maintain my equilibrium, which is so important when taking a leap of faith.

In spring of 2019 I announced a very special school that I would be teaching to a small group of women who would travel to my Vermont cottage four weekends out of the year beginning in spring of 2020. This was a dream I had and I was hoping to eventually build a guest cottage behind the barn and spend my life teaching small groups on that lovely island. My school filled almost instantaneously to where I ended up with three groups of eight women each. The deposits I received helped tremendously toward paying for the renovation.

I had just enough money left to purchase a 2013, three-thousand-dollar Subaru Impreza with over two-hundred and fifty-thousand miles on it. I made the purchase through Craigslist, Vermont, while still living in Redmond and put my trust in my spirit friends that the seller was an honest man. He actually drove it to my cottage in Vermont for me and my contractor kept it at his house till I arrived. And I will quickly say that after my move I found out that I lived just down the street from a retired auto mechanic who worked out of his garage. He had stopped working for the most part but we had a nice connection and when my car needed anything I simply dropped it off and walked home, and he would drop it back to me when he was done with it. My cost was far less than taking it to a regular shop and I didn't have the hassle of needing a ride or having to wait on site. It was another sign that I was in perfect flow.

In June of 2019 I rented a twenty-foot U-Haul, hired professional packers to stuff it to the gills, and with my cat, Socks, and a dearly loved prior retreat client who offered to be my co-pilot, we drove cross-country to my beautiful Vermont cottage. I dropped her at her parent's house in upstate New York, and drove the last few hours on a bright sunny day with views of a sparkling Lake Champlain to my darling cottage on an isle.

I arrived to a bustling group of hardworking men who were busily finishing up the renovation. They said they'd help me unpack the following day so I sat on the back of my moving truck in my driveway and just took in the beauty of my surroundings. Shortly thereafter, a young man from a house across the street came walking over to me with a pint of fresh picked strawberries, welcoming me to the neighborhood. He had a small farm behind his house and invited me to join his CSA, which I did on the spot. Local farms are dear to my heart and I have endeavored since my daughters were young to eat 'as close to the farm as possible'. Well, now the farm was across the street and one house down from me. Pure magic and even more magic to come.

I soon met my amazing neighbors directly across the street who lived in a lovely old Victorian house with a porch laden with red geraniums that contrasted beautifully with their soft grey and white-trimmed house. They were warm, funny women who ran a successful pottery company. They had three cats they lovingly doted on and we became dear friends. They shared with me a story that further lent to the magic

I was experiencing. One of them was from Israel and she was a Faerie woman, there was no doubt. My house had stood empty for a while and she used to look out the kitchen window and say, "A mushroom shaman is going to buy that house. She is from Seattle and we're going to be friends." My jaw just dropped, I was so shocked and her wife said, "Shonagh, she did this almost every day and she was certain it would happen!" My mind blown—I thanked her wholeheartedly for helping me with my spell. These were my people.

Once fully unpacked I was in need of a sofa and comfy chairs and a rug for the living room area. I had a dining table and chairs but I'd given away my other furnishings before moving as I knew I wouldn't be able to get them through the doors to this older house. I figured I'd be able to find something if I shopped around but then I received the final bill from my contractor, so what little money I had left over went to him. I was taking a few weeks off to get settled and explore the area and then I would need something comfortable for my retreat clients to sit on other than a dining room chair. I was in a quandary, when a week later I heard from my oldest and dearest friend I've known since we were sixteen. She knew my situation and she called to say that she was walking with a wealthy friend that morning who told her she had no intention of living in the States again and she had a temperature-controlled storage unit full of antiques and furnishings and she "just wanted to find it a good home." She didn't say she wanted to sell it. She wanted to give it away to a good home. For free.

My friend told her I needed furniture and she asked for my email and sent me photos of the most beautiful furnishings. A few days later I rented a ten-foot Uhaul and drove over four hours to the storage place where I was given a gorgeous curved-back sofa, a pair of tufted chairs, a pair of floor lamps on a braided wood base with silk shades, an oval coffee table, a beautiful tall wardrobe from Provence, a smaller carved wood cabinet from France, two small antique accent tables, a very nice blanket basket from France, two absolutely gorgeous Tibetan wool rugs, 8' x 10' and 9' x 11', a smaller Persian carpet in beautiful colors and a stunning 9' x 11' wool and silk carpet. Just as I was about to leave, she offered me a gorgeous pair of handblown Steuben glass candlesticks that I gratefully accepted.

I felt like I was in a dream and I had to pinch myself. I'd spent about five hundred dollars on the rental truck to pick up many thousands of dollars-worth of exceptionally beautiful furnishings. My friendly contractors came the next day to put the furnishings in place for me. I had a beautiful bay window in the living room that extended out onto the wraparound porch and the sofa fit perfectly in that space. The coffee table was the perfect size for the area as well as the pair of tufted chairs. The two accent tables fit perfectly in two areas where I had noted I would need small tables. The smaller carved cabinet fit perfectly in a nook by the sofa and I placed the Steuben glass candlesticks on top of it. On the living room floor was one of the Tibetan carpets in a soft aqua with a botanical design in soft brown. The finished look was so impressively beautiful and the furnishings so perfectly suited to the scale of the room, you would have thought I'd hired the best New York designer to do the job. My thoughts went to one of my cherished books as a child, *A Little Princess*, by Frances Hodgson Burnett. The main character in that story, a little girl, is banished to live in a cold attic and awakens the following morning to a sumptuously decorated sanctuary of beauty, gifted her by a generous soul.

I stood on the soft Tibetan carpet in the center of my sweet cottage, surrounded by my newly gifted exquisite furnishings and put my hands over my heart, closed my eyes and thanked my good Sidhe for such a lavish gifting. To my utter surprise, because I am not clairaudient, I heard the words, "Welcome home."

The following pages were my instruction manual for setting my sights and going after my dreams.

I Cast This Spell (January 2018)

Woman's breath of fire blows
I call the force that makes seeds grow
Imbue my healing practice, fine
Abundant growth is my design

My good work tends body/mind
Their mental spells, I'll help unbind
Many clients coming now
This year is a 'Holy Cow!'

All my efforts paying off
No more will naysayers scoff
This year brings me fortune, large
My intention sets the charge

This command creates the stage
And brings to me a goodly wage
In turn my work assists these folk
Whose fire within I ably stoke

They come to me to learn and grow
For their desire is to know
How to heal and steer their ship
And how to take a mystic's trip
Into the ethers of the mind
Where wait the teachers of a kind
That lead initiates into knowledge
I can help them find that college

So, to me comes now success
The clients will come in excess
I stand here ready for good times
With kindreds old, I have aligned
My path is sound, my footsteps, sure
My heart guides rightly, it is pure

Thanks be to the spirits, bright
For leading me through this dark night
Now the daylight calls to me
My heart now healed, I walk as free...

Conjuring How To (February 2018)

You're calling in financial gain
Well, we've a message to explain
Dear, everything is energy
A driver that you cannot see
That energy's composed of light
A vibration that's quite the sight
Like water, it travels in waves
And you can get it to behave

Inside your mind conceive of money
And though this may seem quite funny
Transform it into energy
And observe its frequency
Use imagination here
To conjure forth and make it clear

The cash now looks like energy
And you must create synergy
An antennae you now become
Attracting in a steady hum
Of money formed of frequency
That seeks you like a honeybee

Become a magnet like a flower
Energizing in the power
Magnetic waves that define money
They're the bees and you're the honey

Now the charge must build some more
Your emotion opens door
Using electricity
Within your mind let yourself see
The end result that you desire
Your emotion is the fire

Within you that builds the charge
With emotion make it large

Excitement fills you at the thought
Of all the dreams that you have sought
To bring into reality
At this moment you clearly see

Now take yourself upon a tour
Of dream fulfilled, its outcome sure
See inwardly all the details
And know that you have tipped the scales
The odds are on your side this time
The spell cast forth in potent rhyme...

Genie's Lamp (March 2018)

Remember the power within your mind
An ancient spell you now unbind
The negative voices that claim that you can't
Are losing their might, their effects will be scant
For you are a being who hails from the kind
Of folk who can conjure by using the mind

The world as you know it will begin to change
Your mind holds the wand and it will rearrange
The old programs within you are cast out to sea
Watch them flowing away as you feel yourself free
From the bonds of those thoughts that you once felt were real
You access your true nature they tried to steal

Your true nature lives in the temple of mind
It's a genie's lamp hidden and it's quite the find
See it clear in your consciousness, shining and bright
You've been on a long journey, now land is in sight

It is time now to resume an ancient art, bold
Where you, the magician, claim this treasure, old
It's a wand, it's a genie's lamp, hidden in you
The more you think of it the more you'll imbue
In yourself the old magic you've had all along
Hold this vision within you and make your mind strong

An old curse you are breaking, now cast your good spell
Use the power of thinking to break out of hell
See the genie's lamp glowing inside of your mind
Think of what you would like and then easily bind
To the vision, the feeling, the outcome you'd like
If you practice enough, it's like riding a bike

Form a friendship with that treasure that's been revealed
An old tool of magicians that's long been concealed
You now hold it, the genie's lamp, a kind of wand
The more that you use it the more you'll grow fond
Of its power to take you where you want to go
But if you don't use it then you'll never know
What the possible futures before you might hold
The old saying that fortune favors the bold
Is a truism known throughout time for good reason
It's courage and action that changes the season

Rise to the occasion, and play with this tool
You've officially entered a new kind of school
Where the power of imagination is taught
You have opened the door to a new kind of thought
Call the genie within you and share the details
Be clear with your vision and what it entails
Feel the presence of this ancient tutor and friend
Who will walk with you all the way up to the end...

Monday Night Invite (April 2018)

You will come play this weekend
And we will dance with our fair friend
Faerie folk who love you so
We'll play with Daughter Who Knows

We wait patiently for you
When timing's right we will imbue
Your mind with good spells that we cast
To help you raise your vessel's mast
And steer your ship to waters clear
Daughter know, you've naught to fear

Take our hands as we take yours
And steer your ship to magic shores
The Good Folk call you Friday night
To tell you that your future's bright
Though you fret and worry so
We will say you're in the flow
Just be calm and let it come
And then get ready for some fun

You are in a sea of change
It is time to rearrange
The rooms within that mind of yours
Your ship will land on distant shores
We will help you break those spells
That have made your mind a hell
Cast by sorcerers, ancient old
Who stepped inside, though they were told
To keep away, respect our space
Instead, determined to erase
Our folk and our old magic, great
They cast a spell and sealed our fate

You are part of this, dear one
And all the good folk of the Sun
These demons they do dance around
And gloat at treasure they have found
But dear, even old spells must break
Their actions, oh, they will forsake

Though we've receded from the minds
Of many races, many kinds
Of folk who once knew us so well
So many stories they did tell

And though it seems we're gone forever
We advise you, daughter, never
Let yourself forget our folk
Use that good mind to invoke
Along with mushroom magic there
We'll come in with greatest care
And open doors within your mind
Once locked yet now we can unbind
Not only your spell, others too
There will be more than a few
Human beings, fair and wise
Who can see with open eyes
And hearts as well, the good folk, we
The Shining Ones you call the Sidhe

We call you here to us this week
We will give more than a peek
Into our world so beautiful
And daughter, you're most dutiful
You speak our poetry so well
When we hear your voice we swell
With pride, we love to hear the rhythms
Watching magically the prisms
Of your field light up the night
You should know, it's quite the sight!

And so, before you hit the hay
We want you to know today
That we are walking by your side
And your good heart gives us great pride
Don't be so hard on yourself
You are loved by Fae and Elf
Know that in your heart of hearts
Get ready for a brand new start

We are entering your dreams
We are coming through in streams
More poetry you will recite
Until then dear, we bid good night...

Be-Mushroomed Full Moon Message (April 2018)

Let us take care of the rest
We will do what we do best
Hold your talisman with care
Money will come from everywhere

This old magic you know well
Watch as your finances swell
Don't worry how it gets to you
We will give more than a clue

Of how to play the field you're in
Tis the time where you begin
A higher phase of learning here
Your good ship you'll ably steer

And now by candlelight you sit
Dear, you will get the hang of it
Your mind's been changed and activated
We will say we are elated

You are wielding well, your wand
And we are growing very fond
Of who you are and what you do
You've thrown yourself in cauldron's brew

And you are waking many folk
With help from old friends you invoke
There's more of us who will be found
Beneath and on the sacred ground

Of land you'll purchase easily
And you will grace it breezily
We're here to help you with this chapter
You are in a grand hereafter

Know this strongly in your mind
The Holy Grail you're sure to find...

Farmhouse Spell (May 2018)

Where I'll end up, I'm not sure
The choices now are quite a blur
I ask humbly for farmhouse
I'll tend kindly sheep and mouse
Pray give me an orchard, grand
So I can pick my fruit by hand
Veggie and herb gardens too
Lots of berries, more sweet fruit

May the soil be fertile found
I'll be fed by sacred ground
Lots of flowers, many blooms
Can be seen from every room
Of my sweet farmhouse filled with light
I'll feel so good day and night

Wood cook stove in kitchen, warm
I'll be cozy when it storms
Both my girls will love this place
Joyful when they see its face
Many clients will come too
I will have more than a few
Gatherings both large and small
Everyone will have a ball

This, my magic mystic place
Rural farmhouse where the pace
Slows to smell a fragrant flower
And take in my ivy tower
Topiary in my garden
Standing tall where ground has hardened
Cold in winter's snowy weather
Till in summer when the heather
Blankets all in purple blue

Every season is a new
Stage for beauty everywhere
Those who come will sit and stare
Taking in the beauty here
Its effects will make minds clear

I'll tend to its every need
Happily, I'll pull the weeds
Sowing seeds that flourish well
In my garden beauty dwells

Inside my house, a lovely sight
Looking pretty day or night
Wide plank floors and wooden beams
This home's solid to its seams
Wilton carpets made of wool
In the bedrooms, colorful
Super snuggly gorgeous beds
For my guests to lay their heads
Jewel box bathrooms laid with tile
Accessorized with lots of style
Porcelain tub inviting me
To rest and bathe in luxury
Every fixture chose with care
I'll see beauty everywhere

My home will be the perfect size
And very easy on the eyes
The feel of this place calms the mind
Many spells it will unbind
For this place is a faerie's nest
Of all my homes this is the best
My heart will sing when I find this
The ground around it I will kiss...

Farmhouse Spell Cast Forth (June 2018)

Surprise me in the best of ways
Money comes to me these days
From many places, magnetized
Into my field it's realized
Abundance now, my life is rich
I've sown it ably, stitch by stitch
The avenues of flowing wealth
Are giving my bank account health

My farmhouse coming now to me
This sweet place sets my spirit free
I just let go and open wide
And with the keys I'll step inside

In my life, I've changed the tide
With magic from the other side
We work together, Fae and me
They've helped me open eyes to see

So many people I will help
To steer their ships with expert stealth
I'll be protected all the while
Upon me, the good spirits smile

These rhymes are potent that I write
The words hold charge and also might
The Good Folk lead me to the place
Where I access a magic ace
I use with care to cast my spell
To lift good people from their hell

I've arrived at a new shore
So many good things are in store
As I serve beauty everyday

And use my sword of light to slay
The suffering and outworn lies
And help my clients see with eyes

And for myself, my eyes see home
A cottage and a yard to roam
And kindly neighbors with a smile
And friends who'll come and stay awhile

It's on its way, I'll be there soon
When I arrive, my heart will swoon
I must proceed with greatest care
And soon my spell will take me there...

My Spell is Bound (July 2018)

My farmhouse comes now, it is gifted
A place where my spirit's lifted
This sweet home, chosen by they
My gracious friends known as the Fae

A secret kept well out of sight
Until the day when clever sprites
Reveal to me my lovely home
A place where I will live alone
And host good folk from far and wide
And warmly welcome them inside

An energetic, magic land
Soon will be tended by my hand
I've naught to fear, just open wide
And with the keys, I'll step inside

And all the nature spirits, kind
Will cheer with me at such a find
The fireflies will dance around
Because my new home has been found

I now reclaim my magic, old
That I have put forth with a bold
Stroke of faith that it will come
A gathering place for everyone
To come for rest and conversation
And to feel rejuvenation

This home waits until the day
That I arrive from far away
To grace it with a woman's touch
I will love this house so much

This sweet place, a treasure found
Mark my words, the spell is bound!

It's Gifted
(August 2018—I was on an airplane)

You wish from us a farmhouse, dear?
'Twill be our gift for ancient seer
A place to love and steward well
Hold tight dear daughter, soon we'll tell

The stars aligning in the sky
It's coming soon, the time is nigh
Your bank account is growing fast
You will amass a fortune, vast

A windfall on its way to you
This cauldron is a potent brew
You've magnetized a money train
By calling to a higher plane

We're friends of old known throughout time
We inspire your clever rhymes
This place of beauty you will treasure
It will bring you every pleasure

Your good work will flourish there
As you tend your folk with care
You'll decorate with flair and style
The look of it will make you smile

Your lovely daughters will come often
This, a place where spirits soften
Slowing down to take it in
And free the mind from media spin

This place, a nod to simpler times
As gentle breezes stir the chimes
And mountains in the distance, seen
Changing hue from blue to green

How you'll love the quiet there
As you sit in comfy chair
And savor beauty all around
Grateful for this treasure found

It's a promised haven, gifted
Ensuring your spirit's lifted
Birds will sing throughout the day
Until the owls at night hold sway
And many creatures you will see
Thriving in the harmony

It's not long now, be patient, dear
And soon it all will become clear
The place you've called in from your heart
Will bring to you a brand new start...

Endnote—I was in the back of an airplane and closed my eyes for a few minutes after the poem came through. When I opened them there was a woman near my row standing in line for the bathroom. She was wearing a black T-shirt with a message on the front in large white letters and I could only see the top word, which said, "MAKING." As she stepped forward into full view my mouth dropped in shock when I read the entire message on her chest:

MAKING MAGIC HAPPEN

2019 New Year's Message

Dear, you do not need to choose a card
You're thinking that this could be hard
But it's quite simple as you know
Just feel success from head to toe

To you comes a big payday
And you are helped by we, the Fae
You'll draw to you finances, grand
And we will lend a helping hand

This is a year that adds to three
And you'll be financially free
Just keep it up, your good mind's work
Responsibility, you don't shirk

New life will come to you this spring
But in the meantime, do your thing
More people booking retreats soon
You've activated a new Moon

The energetics building now
Dear, as you say, it's 'Holy Cow'
Buckle your seatbelt, sit up straight
This new life promised will be great
You've upped your game from in the past
This New Year brings you wonders, vast
So many here supporting you
This cauldron is a magic brew

You've naught to worry, it's a go
You've raised your sail, the wind will blow
You must now trust we have your back
We will not let those sails go slack

The path is paved, the doors are open
This, the moment you've been hoping
Will occur, success assured
How could it not? Don't be absurd!

Keep your eyes upon the path
You've got this now, you know the math
The talismans will help as well
Your magic strengthens as it swells

As you progress through this year's door
You'll find yourself on higher floors
This year's a good one, lots of luck
You will not be feeling stuck

Just let it flow like poetry
Success is coming, wait and see
You've worked quite hard to make this come
Your efforts bring a mighty sum
Of abundance to your pocket
You will take off like a rocket

It's assured, the stars have spoken
So, we share this little token
Of a message just for you
No more will your good mind stew
That worry goes out with the trash
Replaced with knowing that the cash
Is on its way, the chapter's written
With your life you will be smitten

We can see, we're in the know
You soon will reap the seeds you sow...

Reminder (February 2019)

Make it big, do not hold back
You will not be stuck in lack
This, a golden chance to fly
Be assured success is nigh
Remember dear, it's in your head
So, think of your success instead

That Faerie cottage calling you
In your mind you must imbue
The force of momentum that's vast
This will happen very fast

Keep it up, the work you're doing
We will say this cauldron's stewing
Forces gathering for a spell
This will turn out very well

All the things you have in mind
This, a spell 'twill surely bind
To an outcome that's assured
All that work that you've endured
Will pay off handsomely we say
Success is yours, it's here to stay
We told you dear, it's a new leaf
You can let go of the grief
And the worry and the pain
You work now on a higher plane

The time is now and you are in it
Tell your story, go and spin it
You are funny, sharp and clever
Know that in your mind and never
Fall into that sticky web
It's an old one, let it ebb

And flow away as these things do
You are in a year, brand new

2019 is a 3
You know that's magic, you can see
Charge it, daughter, with your mind
And with emotion you can bind
A spell that changes everything
And when it does your heart will sing

It's here, so start this day with joy
This, the spell you now employ…

Moonlit Scene with Fairies, Margaret Rice Oxley (circa 1920).

Morning Walks

*The color associated with the transcendent state was always green:
the colour of Nature and of Robin's Greenwood garb. It was the
paramount colour of the elves and of the stag of the Caille Daouine,
while also being the Gaels' colour of death. Green is additionally
associated with the goddess Venus and with fertility... It is the color of
wisdom, and the colour of Elphame, both of which are accessible to the
uninitiated...*

– Realm of the Ring Lords, Laurence Gardner

I mentioned in the last chapter that I'd created a school that was to start in May of 2020. We all know what happened in 2020 and so much has changed for all of us since then. I, personally, did not fall into lockstep with the corporate government fear campaign, and my intuition confirmed for me that there was far more going on than meets the eye. My school lost two-thirds of the participants and I witnessed the virus of fear take over the minds of otherwise reasonable people. I took myself off all social media, stopped writing my monthly newsletter, and got the very clear message to "keep your circle small."

Unlike the many people who lost their shirts that year with the draconian shut-downs, I was exceptionally fortunate to continue with a steady stream of determined clients throughout that year and the next, other than the month of April when everyone was home wondering what the hell was going on. The timing of my move to Vermont was not lost on me and I remembered a very wise woman who'd come for a retreat in January of 2019, months before I was to leave the Seattle area. In a be-mushroomed trance state she looked at me and said, "You are leaving this area just in time." I recognized the oracular state of those words and I nodded my head and said, "I know."

I have been listening to astrologist, Robert Phoenix, for over ten years now. In addition to his astute readings, he hosts a show on Youtube and Boxcast where he discusses the astrological movements and their effects on current events. His observations and predictions are as searingly accurate as his individual readings, which I get annually. In the fall of 2019 Robert said that whatever is coming in 2020 and the next few years beyond, it's going to be incredibly intense and will change life as we know it. He essentially said that if we get through these next few years, we'll be high-fiving each other on the other side. This was no joke and I knew to prepare as best I could, particularly in my psyche.

That began a yearly declaration practice that I started in January of 2020 and continue to do at the start of every year. Knowing the shit was going to hit the fan, and knowing that I had a living to make and no partner to step in if needed, I used the power of my mind as I'd been taught all those years to set a touchstone for myself for the year. What immediately came to mind was Geronimo, the great Apache leader and medicine man who eluded capture and death for twenty-five years, no bullet ever touched him. I made the fearless, noble Geronimo my inspiration and pledged that I would sail through whatever battle happened that year, unscathed. This was neither a futile New Year's resolution, nor some pithy New Age sentiment. This was a serious pledge of alignment to the forces of preservation, courage and mental power. I reminded myself of that declaration several times over the course of that year.

I was beyond grateful to have been led to that tiny island in northern Vermont, away from the absolute insanity taking place in the cities in the form of riots, violence, fear, depression and *othering* on steroids. I was in a little sanctuary and had neighbors and friends in the area who were of like mind, and that camaraderie carried me through. As well, I was grateful in more ways than I can count for the grace of having a retreat client, an intrepid good soul in my home every week where we would delve into the depths of their being and explore the richness of the mystery and the beauty of being alive, in spite of the fear propaganda playing out in the greater world. I held firmly to the wisdom of Nature, and in return, She held me in a cocoon of beauty and blessings.

In winter of 2021 my snowy island oasis was next-level cold. I've never experienced minus fifteen below zero weather before and it was to be a reality more than a few times that season. I had a wood stove as my only heat source in the enclosed breezeway of my house, which I used as my bedroom, and a pellet stove was in the living room. I regularly split wood out in the back barn to bring into my bedroom, and I shlepped forty-pound bags of wood pellets into the house for the pellet stove. One cold morning I was walking to the house with an armful of split wood when I slipped on the ice and hit the back of my head. It rang my bell but did no actual harm, fortunately. That said, I had a thought, *How is this going to look for me ten years from now?* I was fifty-eight at the time and my home required a fair amount of tending, which I lovingly did but it was a lot for one person.

I had put in a fifty-by-fifty-foot vegetable garden and 12 fruit trees with the help of my neighbor and friend, Frank, who was a godsend. He mowed my giant yard and raked and burned the unbelievable amounts of leaves around my house in the fall. I tended the garden between 5 and 6:30 am on mornings when I had a retreat client for the week, as well as the flower garden around my house. I also had a sixty-foot diameter, seven-circuit labyrinth put in, made of stone from a dried-up riverbed in Vermont. It was the most beautiful creation and I opened the energies in the center of it with my two lovely friends from across the street. I walked it regularly and tended to the weeds that insisted on pushing through the soil coverings that had been laid by the Druid... Yes, the man who built the labyrinth is a practicing Druid—what a coincidence. I'm laughing as I write this. You can't make this stuff up.

Well, by January of 2022 I was exhausted. My busy schedule had finally caught up with me and for the first three months of that year, I only worked with one retreat client per month instead of my regular schedule of three, usually four booked weeks a month. In mid-January, I had a catch-up Zoom call with a retreat client who had come the prior summer. At that time, I was still hoping to raise the money to build a small guest cottage behind the barn and resume teaching small groups. The money wasn't materializing, which was perplexing, as my big spells seem to take three years and it was time for that to come forward. Herein, was an important teaching I received on working magically. Guess what? You don't have the last word! Always remember that! There was good reason why that guest cottage was not to be, but I'm in a body on the stage of life and I don't have the script for the next act.

My client on the Zoom call, a gentleman from Maine, told me he'd spoken to his psychic about me the other day. I asked why and he said he was thinking of gifting me some money to start the guest cottage and when he broached it with his psychic, she told him I would be moving. He told her that was impossible, that I loved that house, but she replied that the cold was getting to me and she saw me in one of the southern states like North or South Carolina or Tennessee. I looked at him mutely, I didn't know what to say and he said, "I'm just the messenger." After the call I discussed it with a friend who suggested I not be attached to the house and simply take the weekend to look into those states to see if there is even a remote interest in that possibility.

I made an appointment with my friend, Diana, who has been reading Lenormand cards since her teens. She is the best of the best and has been reading for me accurately for almost fifteen years. I trusted her guidance implicitly so we looked at the possibility in her cards. Just as I had already decided in my mind, the cards were a 'no' to those three states. I knew a great lady in Virginia who had done work with me in the past and so I asked Diana what the cards had to say about that state. Well, they were beautiful and she said I would be very happy there but to know that if I put my cottage up for sale it would sell very quickly so be ready.

I was getting more curious about the possibility of moving to a warmer clime and I emailed my Virginia friend to ask her where I should look in that state. She owned a gorgeous alpaca farm by the Shenandoah mountains and her response shocked me. She wrote, "You can live here." Well, I'd seen photos of that farm and I replied, "That would be dreamy." She wrote back, "I would love it." Now, I was really confused. I wrote and asked, "Are you just playing around here or are you serious?" She replied, "Dead serious." We proceeded to have a number of conversations and she told me she'd thought earlier about the possibility of me living on the farm but I was so wed to Vermont she figured it would never happen. Now that I was open to it, we discussed the possibility of helping her with a few interesting future projects. I was very excited at the thought of collaborating with someone as creative and brilliant as she is and six weeks later, I drove ten hours to see the farm and spend a few days with her and her husband.

It was blustery cold when I visited in mid-March but I could imagine how beautiful the place would look in the spring. My host showed me the 1905 cottage I could live in, and gave me a little tour of the area. The setting was perfect for my retreats. I would be all tucked away and yet central to everything, which I was ready for. When I returned to Vermont, I knew I was to move. I had the distinct feeling while in Virginia that there was something very important waiting for me in that state. As well, I pay attention to the little signs along the way. This woman and I share a love and appreciation for owls, which have been a guiding light for me since I began working with the mushrooms. And the little town I would be living in is named after a hill and the word, *sidhe,* of course, means 'mound' or 'hill'.

I realized that I had been brought to the sanctuary island of Isle La Motte as a means of protection during the onslaught of the Covid years. I felt I was destined to steward that cottage and install a labyrinth on the land that would radiate subtle harmonizing energies for a long time to come.

I got my house packed up over a few months and had the exterior painted. The couple who purchased it walk labyrinths, which was another crazy 'coincidence', so it worked out beautifully. I made the money back that I'd put into the house after the sale, which gave me a foundation on which to start this new chapter. I walked the labyrinth a final time and said good-bye to the spirits of that land and thanked them for all they'd given me and all they'd taught. I felt closure with the house and it wasn't until I said good-bye to Frank and his sweet wife that I began to cry. They had been so good to me while I lived there, as had my dear friends across the street. There was a cast of characters on that island that I could write a book about someday, and they all hold a special place in my heart.

I moved to Virginia in early June of 2022 and this is my favorite state I've ever lived in. I spent more time with my daughters in my first summer here than in three years in Vermont because, of course, I was quite off the beaten track there, which was the idea for that time. Here, I am accessible to my cherished daughters and the lovely people who come for their retreats. A very special element here is the proximity to the

Shenandoah Mountains, which are a ten-minute walk from the house. Almost daily, I do a brisk, five-mile walk along the base of those green mountains that are dotted with black Angus cows and horses, and my heart is soothed.

I am in a state of grace on those early morning walks where the beauty of the surrounding landscape brings me into balance and clarity for the day. I tune into the subtle frequencies of Nature and absorb the soft rays of the rising Sun. This is cherished time alone where I can sort my thoughts and talk to the spirits. I never bring my cellphone, as I don't want that radiation machine against my body, so instead I bring my digital recorder in case I want to record an idea or task, etc. Like my runs in the past, I am in a mild alpha state on those walks and I let myself daydream and enjoy the present moment.

In fall of 2022 I had three days in a row where a poetic transmission came through on my morning walk. All three times I was walking between a tunnel of trees along a hill in the road. As trees are natural antennae's I have wondered since if that area is especially tuned to a frequency that is conducive to a very mild trance state. I am always aware of those particular trees and will often send words of prayer into the area. On the day the first message came through I was in thoughts of concern about the ever-widening encroachment of technology and what it is doing to our world. I was thinking about the darker agendas behind it and I asked aloud that the forces of good put a stop to tyranny. In came an answer in pure poetry and I spoke it into my recorder.

I got home and transcribed the message and stored it in a folder. It was at that time that I was thinking of putting some of my earlier poetic messages to music and imagery in an effort to put them out there to those who would be touched by their message. I thought this particular transmission would be especially relevant at this time. The following morning, I took off down the road for my walk and as I approached the tunnel of trees, I was thinking about what it is to have faith and that I would need it in this next chapter. To my surprise, in came a beautiful treatise on the subject of faith. Reading it through at home after transcribing, I felt great comfort in the wisdom of the prose. I made a note to include that message in my poetry videos.

As I know well the rhythm of the three, I couldn't help but wonder if another message would come through as I left the house for my morning walk. My mind soon fell into wandering as it does on these forays. As I was considering the addictive nature of our devices that are all too ubiquitous now, I was also questioning what could possibly assist us at this time. As if in conversation with the invisible realms an answer flowed in once again, poetically, and I dictated the words into my recorder. In came what I've titled, Call On Grace, the words of which brought me some peace. Grace itself is a profound mystery and very much a real event that happens in the most extraordinary ways.

I like to look up words in Webster's 1828 dictionary, as the older dictionaries far exceed the newer, dumbed down versions in depth of word meanings. Old Webster has more than a few definitions of grace but the one that caught my eye says,

> Appropriately, the free unmerited love and favor of God, the spring and source of all the benefits men receive from Him.

Grace is inextricably connected to the infinite love of the source of all life, whether we call that God, Allah, Creator, the One, it speaks to the highest order creationary force that has the power to gift us in infinite ways, as in 'it will take an act of God to save us'. That act is a force of love, which is the power to affect individuals and the world at large in times of havoc, destruction, devastation, etc. Coupled with faith, it is what sees us through. We could think of it as a mindset, one that enables certain people to persevere while others with no such connection might falter.

Well, I hoped for another message on day four and of course it was not to be. I like to say that this isn't 'instant coffee' though when the gates are open it sure feels like that. However, I cannot pour forth these messages, willy-nilly everyday and post them on Instagram. They come in when the time is right and I am expected to sit with the message and ponder its meaning for me, and then put it into practice in whatever way is needed. These messages have been my guideposts these past many years and they have helped me immensely with my doubt and fear, and my limited thinking that has much improved thanks to this connection.

And of course, my connection to the Otherworld has deepened and ripened over time like a true, enduring friendship.

I did receive another poem on a walk a couple of months later when I was on my way to visit the Faerie tree. I discovered this dramatic-looking tree in a field at the end of one of my walks and I was struck by its regal beauty. It has a feel to it that is distinctive and it catches my attention every time I walk in its vicinity. The poem came through while standing at the fence admiring the tree and as I continued my walk home it followed me, as it were, and a sweet tale of devotion flowed through me till I reached my destination.

The following transmissions are a blend of sobering counsel, encouragement, instruction and levity.

Counsel from the Green Realms

Spirits wise, I ask you please
Bring the dark ones to their knees
Wake the people from their slumber
Or they will see they're just a number

Answer

Full Moon lights what has been hidden
From the shadows, what's forbidden
Now has voice through those devices
Note the core of that word, 'vices'

This is yet another warning
Many of you will be mourning
What's been lost to screen time's call
It encourages the fall
Of mind from sovereignty's embrace
Gone is reason without trace

An overlay of frequencies
That ensure that you won't be free
Yet like good midwife, Nature waits
Align with her to mitigate
The sticky web of 'intern—net'
Whose spell causes you to forget
Where you come from
What gives you life
She cuts through deceit like a knife

As your ancestors once knew
You must follow Nature's cue
Nature's systems don't abuse
In Nature there's no evil ruse

Imperiled are they who ignore her signs
Those who do soon become blind
For false systems lead one astray
Stealing cherished rights away

Nature's laws are easily learned
Long has man heeded the turn
Of starlit wheel that marks the times
Of darkness or of light, sublime

The coming tide calls you away
From those devices that hold sway
Instead, attention must be drawn
Toward taking you from lowly pawn

To king or queen on chessboard's face
With that mindset you will erase
The sense of powerlessness you feel
The dark masters want you to kneel
Before their mighty creations
They want control of every nation
In you dwells the Holy Spirit
Be still and quiet and you'll hear it
Inner voice speaks without sound
Yet most ignore it, they are bound
To wrong-held beliefs put in them
By clever bards who spew their phlegm

Before this cycle of challenge ends
You'll witness many strong wills bend
To march in lock-step with the rest
You've witnessed many fail the test

Only when one's will is strong
Can one resist urge to belong

Initiations are not easy
They will call you to the floor
It's when our hero's on his knees he
Finds the secret hidden door
That leads to inspiration's light
That offers ways to tame the night

An inborn navigation tool
Takes you beyond deception's rule
The hidden genius is now found
Whose tools will help to break new ground...

Faith

That word, 'faith' has your attention
We will give it more than mention
As you say, it's a mystery
There's so much in your history
Of souls whose strong faith saw them through
We wish to impress this on you

Since early childhood you've known us
You know our guidance you can trust
In lifetimes past you did just that
We always know where you are at

For this next chapter, hold our hands
For you are loved by shimmering band
Of radiant beings so few know
We live within the steady flow

Of time that frames your earthly walk
Together, we will ably stalk
The timeless gem of wisdom's light
Once grasped in mind it stems the blight

Of foolish thoughts that plague your mind
A hard-won gem for those to find
Good counsel to you we'll deliver
'Twill be like arrows in your quiver

You're protected this go-round
Solutions will be easily found
You will share with those who hear
Your words will help them quell their fear

Like bagpipes that led warriors, brave
The right words spoken well will save

The ones who hear from falling prey
To all the lies that rule your day

And that will strengthen their resolve
And many a problem will be solved
One must have faith that this can be
Be resolute and you will see
What you call miracles will occur
When heart and mind are deeply stirred
The forces form to what you vision
How you think is your decision
Call us in to help you steer
Your sturdy ship to waters, clear

Every hero has a sage
Whose wisdom guides him to engage
The trials of life that test one's mettle
When faith is strong it serves to settle
Doubts and fears that always test
They'll undermine the very best

If one has no faith to be found
Tis like a forest with no sound

Faith is like a mighty sword
That steadies you, pushing you toward
Whatever goal that is held, dear
Faith is the enemy of fear

Hold the lantern high for others
They will see what has been covered
The Holy Grail is found in mind
The hero's quest serves to unbind
The web of old beliefs and thoughts
Once cast out they reveal what's sought

Have faith and call to we, your guides
Together we will ably ride
The waves of this oncoming tide
You'll feel our presence by your side

We'll whisper softly in your mind
And interrupt those thoughts that bind
The genius in you will be stirred
And you will rise above the herd
To walk a path that few will take
Your faith endures, make no mistake

For you have found your way to friends
Who've walked with you through many trends
And this lifetime you hold a wand
That represents a timeless bond

That entwines our good hearts with yours
Out ships are tethered to your shores...

Call On Grace

Energetic tentacles reaching out through plasma screen
Holds the mind in manacles, the virus sits within, unseen
If unchecked it directs you away from sovereignty, imbued

The mind's a reflection of Source
Some are soft and others, course
As a coin contains two faces
So, the mind for every race is
Influenced by what it hears
And sees, and loves, and hates and fears

A powerful wand when directed well
Creating on Earth heaven or hell
Sages through time have known its power
Sharing wisdom with each hour

Your earthly clock strikes twelve again
Beyond that, a new timeframe
A new cycle starts with one
Behold, the changes have begun

If your mind is not your own
You are not unlike a clone
That mimics what it has been shown
Within a test tube it's been grown

Held from Nature's influence
Poisoned with a confluence
Of experiments upon the mind
The soul is chained to sorcerer's bind

This time calls on mental power
To bring wisdom to the hour
You fear that it's not enough, to influence those captured souls
This is where the wand of Faith is activated by the bold

We urge you now to wield that sword
When you have Faith, it leads you toward
All that you need to greet the hour
Faith held strong will give you power

The body responds to the mind
Your thoughts form a spell that binds
Activate the genius within
Creatively design your spin
That counteracts pervasive spells
To take you out of sorcerer's hell

You've heard of those stories told
Of folks who rose to moment, bold
When faced with an emergency
From their conditioning they broke free
And triumphed over situation
Grace took the wheel within their nation

Grace is more than you realize
Grace is God's love undisguised
Grace cares not for convention
Grace gifts you with bold inventions

Grace comes when you least expect
Hold the Faith and you'll connect
In ways that you would never think
Would save you when you're on the brink
Of dangerous situation there

Grace will help you all to bear
Witness to so-called miracles
Providing for all, empirical
Evidence of what can be
When mind's unbound, open and free

And so with Faith, dear, call on Grace
And She'll illuminate that space
Between your ears and in your heart
When inner light shines bold, you'll start

To realize possibilities
This is when you'll ably seize
The day, as the old saying goes
You will face the earthly woes
And cast your light in unique ways
We watch you and count the days
Till the time comes when minds are free
A whole new world will come to be...

Faerie Tree

I walk this windy morning, strong
My good legs carry me along
Over hill and down again
I walk swift and feel no pain

Making my way to special place
Excited, I quicken the pace
For down the road aways from me
There stands a noble Faerie tree

Alone it stands on open land
As I approach it extends hand
Touching my heart and then my mind
I commune with Faeries, kind

For this tree houses an old race
Hidden deep beneath its face
This tree's a beauty standing there
A living sculpture, branches bare

For now is winter, time to rest
Till spring calls forth milk from breast
Of Mother Nature who will nourish
Her good land so it will flourish

The base of this good tree has there
A Faerie doorway that I swear
Is calling me to come on in
And feel the tree beneath its skin

Good Faerie tree, you've stirred my soul
When I walk by you, I feel whole
Your countenance has dignity
You stand in open field so free

Your beauty is not casual
You look there far from usual
I recognize your quiet soul
I see that you are very old

How I long to sit by you
And hear the stories known to few
Good Faerie folk beneath you live
And to me they have much to give

So many pass you without thought
Away they go, they just cannot
Slow down and behold Nature's form
A sculpture that boldly adorns
An open field of herbs and grass
Good tree, I toast you with my glass
Raised high to toast you in good health
That will come *to* you in great wealth

That field around you shining bright
I can feel it day and night
Good Faerie tree, I give my thanks
When I walk past, I lose my angst

And feel your subtle energy
You shine like beacon so I see
And recognize this Faerie tree
I bid God's grace and love to thee

I welcome you into my dreams
A nightly discourse where it seems
That I'm in an alternate land
Where I hold court with shining band
Of Faerie folk who've known me long
I recognize them by their song
Their music heard at special times

They sing to me in rhythmic rhyme
To ensure our connection's strong

I walk Earth now but I belong
To gracious race of shining Sidhe
Of whom I hold a memory
Of dancing in a forest, green
Moss everywhere on pathways seen

I curtsy to the Faerie Queen
A fairer face I've never seen
The Faerie King extends his hand
Inviting me to Faerie land

Where I will dance into the night
Surrounded by the good folk, bright
All this inspired by good tree
Home to noble shining Sidhe

All this seen on walk this morn
Almost home, I feel reborn
I see with greater clarity
The good farmland that surrounds me

The turkey vultures and the crows
Fly high above, I lift my nose
And inhale scent of morning Earth
That holds the roots of trees whose girth
Is ever-widening with each year
The Sun is shining crystal clear

Ready for another day
I hold the magic of the Fae
As hawk calls out unto its mate
I have found a Faerie gate

Tomorrow's walk I will return
For there is more I want to learn
From gracious Faerie king and queen
Unto their fine realm I have been...

Titania Lying Asleep, Arthur Rackham, 1908.

Mushroom Realm Transmissions

> *I will set out on foot*
> *to the gate I will come,*
> *I will enter the hall,*
> *My song I will sing...*

– Taliesin pen Beirdd

What I am sharing in this final series of transmissions came through via one of the oldest shamanic practices in the world. It involves the ingestion of a plant, fungi, or ritual drink to take the individual into the Otherworld to connect with the intelligences and return with prophecy, counsel and secret knowledge either held within the confines of a priestly class or shared with the community.

The poet initiates of the ancient Celts engaged in a practice called incubation where they would lie in total darkness during daylight hours, and this continued for the duration of their instruction. In the bardic system of learning, it was in darkness where vision and inspiration were sought, as this was akin to the chthonic realm of the underworld. The time of instruction began after the harvest when the days became short and the nights long so that the student would be in continual darkness through the season until they heard the call of the first cuckoo in spring. As the cauldron symbolized the transformative darkness of incubation, it was in this darkness where the poets pondered their given assignments. Within this container they 'stewed' their emotions into poetry to be recited upon their emergence after dusk. The womb-like cauldron compares to the womb of bright Brighid, keeper of the forge and muse of the Irish poets. To them, the cauldron was Her womb, birthing their fully formed prose after gestation in darkness.

The 'classroom' was a small windowless 'house of darkness', and Martin Martin, who wrote of the Scottish Gaelic bardic school, said the initiates wrapped plaids around their heads and placed a rock over their belly. The belly, in Gaelic, the *broinn*, was essential to this practice where deep meditation was maintained through breath control. To assist with breathing from the lower belly, a weight on that area was used in the form of a rock. In his book *A God Who Makes Fire*, author Christopher Scott Thompson surmises it would also help the initiate to project his voice from the abdomen once the 'cauldron of incubation' was activated within him. In his *Description of the Western Islands of Scotland* (1716), Martin Martin wrote, "They shut their Doors and Windows for a Day's time, and lie on their backs with Stone upon their Belly, and Plads about their Heads, and their eyes being cover'd they pump their Brains for Rhetorical Encomium or Panegyrick; and indeed they furnish such a Stile from this Dark Cell as is understood by very few."[49]

The first cuckoo's call was met with mournful resistance, and poet Tadhg Óg Ó Huiginn wrote, "O ye who were in his house and sought art and residence, well might it be hateful to you to hear the utterance of the cuckoo."[50] The Irish poets were loathe to leave these houses of darkness, and Caitlin Matthews writes, "Irish poets before the 18th century regarded it strange for any poet to compose while walking or riding about outdoors so ingrained was this tradition of seeking darkness."[51]

Various forms of incubation were practiced in the ancient world from northern Europe to Greece and Rome. A cave or tomblike chamber served as the ritual space where the initiate would take the inward journey to the lower world. This was a metaphorical death and the origins of this practice go far back in time. The initiate's return from the underworld represented a rebirth whereupon he/she carried the treasured gifts of knowledge, wisdom and understanding. In some of these initiatory practices it is likely that a psychoactive brew of some sort was taken before the descent. As well, worshippers often spent the night at a temple, seeking oracular knowledge from the deity while in total darkness.

The latter years of training for the poet initiates focused on the magical arts. Here, they learned the 'three illuminations' known as Imbas Forosna, Teinm Laegda and Dichetul do Chennaib. According to author/scholar Caitlin Matthews, Imbas means, 'fullness of knowledge, and Forosna translates to 'great kindling,' so this was the cultivating of inspiration, knowledge and mysticism. Teinm Laegda means to gnaw at the pith (the soft, spongy center of a fruit or plant). In this case, the pith was the poem itself where the poet formed a spiraling poem like a fractal that could cast a spell or reveal hidden information. Dichetul do Chennaib was what we call psychometry today. The poets used the whorls on the bottom of their fingers to touch a subject of interest and glean the information they sought. They also used their staffs for this purpose. These exquisitely-trained individuals held in their minds and hearts an extraordinary artistry that is unparalleled today. The mind is a fertile well of infinite possibility, and though bereft of this depth of training now, we can glean inspiration and endeavor to expand ourselves through study and various states of expanded consciousness.

Terrence McKenna famously advised taking mushrooms "alone, in silent darkness," which is what I have been doing for many years now. Though it is hardly the practice of incubation it does echo the ritual descent into the underworld realms in darkness, isolated from others and wholly consumed by Nature's teaching fungi. Like so many others who engage the mushrooms respectfully, I return with insight, deeper knowledge and understanding. I also return with poetry, which I am sharing through this book. I don't write like that naturally, only when I am in an inspired state as I spoke of earlier. I go into the realms when I am called, which in these last several years hosting retreats, is once or twice annually. Each and every time, I enter the realms with humble heart, seeking wisdom. I prefer to be alone in the comfort of my bed and other than the sounds of Nature, I do not like to listen to any music or chanting while on my journey. I think many people are so over-stimulated they fear their own silence yet I find that it is in the silence where I can finally hear my own rhythms.

For as much as I have shared in this book with regard to the poetry, I have much more stored away that is deeply personal and it remains for myself alone. That said, I am quite open with most of what comes through, for if I think a message is relatable to others and potentially helpful in some way then I am happy to bring it forward. The most notable theme these transmissions illuminate for me is hope. Our entire world has become so distorted and what we call leadership is a deplorable spawn of corrupted, black-hearted filth. It is easy to fall into hopelessness and despair but when I read even one of these transmissions, it's as if a spell breaks, and I feel the spark of life's fire reignite in my deepest core. It's like getting a reboot to the psyche.

There is a consistent message flowing throughout the transmissions urging us to remember our true essence, which comes from within and is held beneath the many layers of beliefs, biases and programming that bar access to the higher realm of mind. It's there though, and like Excalibur it can be extracted from the stone after we have cleared away all that has clouded the truth of who we are. Certainly, the plants and fungi can provide us with an effective assist to access the Holy Grail within the mind.

And so, I present you with specific journey transmissions whose poetry I hope will speak to you in profound ways that will lift you up, deliver inspiration, and even at times make you laugh.

Winter Solstice Mushroom Journey (2016)

We are a small conglomeration
Members of the Faerie nation
We would like to sit with you
And offer up our point of view
We have much to say, it's true
We will ensure that you'll construe
Our message to you at this hour
To you, dear one, we will shower
Using words, we like to play
It's the nature of the Fae

Tonight, you'll play with we, the Fae
We'll make your worries go away
Invite us in so we can stay
Awhile and with our good friend, play

Magic we will make tonight
With you hidden out of sight
In your bedroom chamber, dark
Listen and then you will hark

In we come through golden spine
Taking you to place, divine
Hidden deep inside your mind
We will show you how to find
The hidden door, we'll open wide
We'll all together step inside
This will be a pleasant ride
As we speak to you inside

Hard to get you out to play
You would far prefer to stay
All alone with those sad thoughts
We do not like to see you caught

In that web of frequency
We are here to wrest you free

Trust us daughter, this the night
The perfect evening for a flight
The sky is clear, the weather, sure
Your ship that grows in cow manure
Will take you far tonight, dear one
You, a daughter of the Sun

You don't need to eat that much
Just enough so we can touch
The beauty place within your heart
This, the place we like to start

Luring you with Pan's embrace
He puts a smile onto your face

Do not lose heart, good daughter, wise
We do hear your worried cries
Remember, we're a frequency
A current that you cannot see
A separate world, where wise ones, we
Extend our hand to help you free
Yourself from mental prisons there
We seek to make you quite aware
That there is far more here for you
We'll help you with all that you do…

Ancient Shining Ones did walk
On this green Earth, we had our flock
Feel the cauldron in heart center
Placed there by your ancient mentors
No, we are not kin by blood
We showed up after the flood
We cast a magic overlay

Upon the land on which we lay
Upon the land so we the Fae
Would have a place where we could stay
Knowing there would come the day
When dark winged ones would come to slay
The Shining Ones you call the Fae

Yes, dear we're very much alive
And we are sharpening the knives
Of minds like yours preparing you
To walk through veils to join a few
Old friends who've been watching you
While you create that cauldron's brew…

Elfin queen, fair lady there
I am trying not to stare…

You've already 3 books done
Now get ready for some fun
3 more coming soon to you
Muses gift, you are imbued

Priestesses fair, were once everywhere
So many climbed the ancient stairs
Now so few, so few who come
Those who do seek respite from
The stench of pain that lives here now
They have defiled the sacred cow

We imbue the ones with ears
We will gently help you steer
Your ship to waters with skies clear
Away from those dark ones you fear
They really cannot hurt you dear
The more you learn of sovereignty
The better off that you will be

That is when you will be free

And the many that you see
Caught in net they are not free
Yes, they suffer terribly
You do your best to help them see
And if they're lucky, hopefully
They'll catch the drift and sail to seas
That won't produce the storms and gales
The crying, moaning and the wails

The only whales you'll likely hear
Will be the ones that swim quite near
Our ships for they are curious
For we don't cause injurious
Effects upon their sacred waters

This a place where sons and daughters
Mothers fathers and the old
Live in peace and with hearts, bold
They share the light within their soul

This a safe place to behold
Not a dream, dear, it can be
If you open eyes to see
We are playing words with thee
Hoping your good mind will free
Itself from all those thoughts that bind

You must trust and do not doubt
All that worry drains you out
Do not give it any clout
Your heart's divine, now put it out
Into the world to call them thus
Oh daughter, do not make a fuss
With all that doubt, you must stop now

This poetry will teach you how
To use that good mind like a wand
And when you do, you'll grow quite fond
Of all the magic you can make
It lives in you, make no mistake

Love up your beauty girls, divine
You must make more special time
With those good hearts of which you bore
Make good memories, they'll be stored
Within their hearts so they will know
Their mother's love, it will not go
That's because you love them so
Those darling girls, their hearts do glow

Message from the Elfin queen
Love your family, sight unseen
That includes us, daughter dear
Like those girls you wish were near
We too like to bask in love
That your heart has so much of...

We are an Earth race
We are older than time
This planet is our home, sublime
Those who dare destroy its face
They must be more than disgraced
They must be stopped, that sordid lot...

Elf and Fae are similar races
Ancient folk of many faces
Here to help you break old spell
That has made this good Earth hell
A hell that we'd never conceive
This Earth is caught within a weave
Spun by those who do deceive

Yet we say on this magic eve
The darkness ends tomorrow morn
The wolf in sheep's clothes will be shorn
The world will see this evil ruse
And then there will be no excuse

We, the folk of fairy kingdom
Many places that we hail from
This our home from ancient times
We call on Earth to realign
The sleeping ones must wake up now
It makes us sick to see them bow
Before their masters, that cruel race
This is an utter disgrace

We declare this solstice eve
A new Earth we will help conceive
A current that will activate
Its energy will enervate
The green realms rise to the occasion
Activating every nation

We vow that this spell will break
And when it does all will forsake
The sorcerers whose plague has raped
We will not let them escape
They are cowards through and through
When they're dead we will renew
The Earth in every way we can
We are Nature and we span
This earthly sphere where we abide
And we are finished with this ride

And so good souls who are awake
Kindreds we do not forsake
Let us work together now

And we will teach you well, just how
To help the Earth to breathe again
We'll help her heal from all that pain
The wicked ones, they will be slain
We'll lend our power to the sane
Starve the wicked ones, we must
They'll pay dearly for their lust
This, our vow this solstice night
We will ensure this Earth shines bright...

Lady elfin queen, your grace
How I long to see your face
My hand extended into yours
I welcome you onto my shores
Good sister, yes, we'll work together
Sisters throughout any weather
We can find each other's light
Despite how dark becomes the night
Thank you for the gifts so kind
You have opened up my mind
I resisted like I do
But you simply wouldn't shoo

Seducing me with luscious Pan
Pretending well to be my man
The elfin are a beautiful race
Who once held sway upon this place
Your kindness always touches me
Though your face I cannot see
Still, I feel you presently

And at this moment I feel we
Are on the precipice of change
And so, let's work to rearrange
The thinking of our earthly folk
Tonight, with power I invoke

The kind magicians, Elf and Fae
I call in the Sidhe today

I call our magic presently
As we encircle here to see
Our way through this evil spell
We will make this planet well
All the magic Nature holds
This, the time to become bold

Timeless forces that make beauty
Timeless forces, it's your duty
Call the sleeping from the spell
I call the Lady of the Well
With humble heart I call to thee
You, good lady of the Sidhe
Hear me now, this gentle plea
We must help Earth's people see

You, good folk who can invoke
Forces I don't doubt will poke
A hole in that dark bubble there
Their spell of woe with its despair
Must disappear into thin air
As we invoke
Electric current, traveling fast
Through waters vast

The green realms where good folk abide
I humbly call you to my side
And I, a warrior on pages white
Cast poetry that stems this blight
That activates the codes within
To counteract the ghastly sin
Of what happens when mankind falls
And no longer heeds the call

Of Mother Nature, a good friend
Who'll love and love until the end
Of time when she can give no more
How very sad to see that door
Close firmly and with punctuation
'Twill be felt by every nation

So, we must avoid that scene
This is why I call realms, green
To circle round on solstice night
So we can get this planet right
I know the magic lives in me
I was told, I am the trees
I am the forest that was cleared
By agencies that sought to steer
My people from their place of beauty
They enslaved them into duty

I am that forest that was raped
Not a single tree escaped
This, revealed on solstice night
This the darkest before bright
Returns and slowly lights the way
Coaxing life back to the day
Tonight, a potent time for spells
Cast to make this planet well

So, good people of the Sidhe
I know that you will expertly
Put forth what will have to be
In order that Earth's folk will see
The spell must break so harmony
Can reign once more so Earth is free

That's when my kindred's face, I'll see
The elfin queen remarkably

Feeding me this poetry
This, the reason I was seen
When I stood in Scotland, green
Within those circles, ancient old
My frequency was shining bold

I've a key inside of me
Gifted me by elfin queen
Elf and Fae, they are a race
That's lived so long upon this place
They can't imagine anywhere else
This the home of Fae and Elf
And earthly folk who once knew well
Those races, in their tales they'd tell
Of meeting with that special folk
Fires of wisdom they did stoke
Magic too, they'd sometimes share
With those they knew would act with care...

This night has been quite a journey
No, I won't leave on a gurney
Yes, I stalled and hemmed and hawed
And now I lie here very awed
By what's ensued, please feel my thanks
You have lifted all my angst

Dear elfin queen
My shores are yours
I welcome you with all my stores
Of love and generosity
Our love has the ferocity
Of dragons that will throughout time
Delivers us to place sublime...

Woman's breath of fire blows
I speak now as Daughter Who Knows

This spell I cast on solstice night
This spell it holds tremendous might
I cast it now with Elf and Fae
True royalty will have its day
In court, to play with pesky words
And though some might think that's absurd
I feel the heat of dear one's hands
Within my own, this shimmering band
Of beings so rare, so beautiful
The forces will be dutiful

I call an end to this dark night
That for so long has beenEarth's plight
I call the day now to the night
On winter solstice, I, of sight
Do see the gathering forces here
Ready to save this earthly sphere
These are earthly forces, dear
The ones that for long have lived here

We now claim this place so dear
And so it goes, this spell I steer
Cast by a humble ancient seer
I cast out the woe and fear
I call beauty back to stay
And send the dark winged ones away
To twist and burn in their demise
This, I see through seer's eyes
Spell now cast with magic words
I know my spell it has been heard

Forces I have humbly called
I release you one and all
To cast your magic done with care
So that the spell breaks everywhere
So that our good folk wake and know

Remembering so they can grow
A healthy forest on this Earth
That we will steward as it births
An age of reason, wisdom's light
That brings to bear all that is right...

Winter's Night Journey (2018)

Deep in trance, we have you now
This one is a holy cow
We'll deliver you your rhyme
You will get it in good time
We are seated next to he
Pussycat, he likes the Sidhe
Faeries, we do gather here
Pussycat likes to be near
Purring loudly next to you
And so good cat, we will imbue
Your soul as well with Faerie light
This will be a special night

You can feel the resonance
Tonight, you'll with the Faeries dance
In your circle all alone
You've got us on the telephone

Not a dose you often take
It has made you quite awake
Trust, dear daughter, as you say
More to be revealed today

In a safe place once again
Dancing on the earthly plane
Daughter dear, you do complain
Thinking your pursuit's in vain
No dear, feel us in your heart
Opening precious door to start
What you might call a new mindset
One that you won't soon forget

Yes, it's been forgotten here
And we are resurrecting seers

Eyes to see and ears to hear
And not to fall into old fears
Changing history, you could say
Calling now a higher play

We don't like that thing at all (my digital recorder)
Packs a punch, though it is small
Yet you hold it in your hand
Yes daughter, we understand
You are recording here again
On this curious earthly plane

We know you long for sweet connection
We read in your heart, rejection
Daughter know, it's in the past
This good Earth is truly vast
Many potentials here for you
No more will your heart feel blue

We are full of clever quips
And exclaim through your good lips
As you scribe the situation
You record it in your nation
Many here who heard your call
Here to help you, one and all

Breaking heart is no small matter
We represent a grand hereafter
That can be felt while you're alive
A worthy thing for you to strive
To bring beyond the gates of heart
To help, to heal, to birth the start
Of something gracious on this Earth
You'll experience this birth

A bit of advice for you, dear

As we read this body here
Watch the bread it slows the mind
Those grains you use, they were designed
At one time they would take you far
But now be careful in this hour
Those grains, they can harm that body
This is more than being naughty
Oh, and awful sugar there
Daughter, you must be aware
Leave that alone now, let it go
Another evil you won't sow
We are growing healthy gardens
Ensuring arteries don't harden
We are part of your rich soil
Where you good-heartedly toil

Pausing now this vulgar thing
Where on earth is the gold ring?
This you hold in your hand now?
This, you call the sacred cow?
(Laughing)
We laugh at such nonsense there
And still we tell you, be aware
The true intelligence is found
Beneath you in the holy ground
The Earth, a metaphor for you
And so do not be so confused

Machines can do a lot, it's true
But don't think they can replace you
Though certain folks among you think
That they are on the very brink
Of time when their inventions birth
Synthetic forms upon the Earth

It is time to break their spell

This place has become a hell
All the needless suffering
All the good earthly beings
Deserve better, that is so
Got that, dear Daughter Who Knows?

Take that to your listeners there
Help them to become aware
As you did playing with A.I.
A eye.
An eye that watches you
And with cunning it does brew
An ugly cauldron in its wake
That's a spell you all must break

As your kitty cleans his fur
So must you, dear, please transfer
Into the living world of beauty
Take that as your sacred duty

Vast mysterium of light
Many prisms, quite the sight
There is much you've not been told
Yet you hold it, ancient old
In your living body there
Yet sadly, most are unaware

We do not seek to possess
For if we did, 'twould be a mess
We simply offer our good counsel
Take it all or just an ounce will
Satisfy, yes just a drop
In your mind we're like a mop
That can absorb the detritus
And sweep aside nevertheless
And help you *birth*—an over-used word

But do not think that it's absurd

We're opening doors that once were shadowed
Opening the ground that's hallowed
That's been hidden, well cared for
Time to open up that door

It will take more than an hour
For our folk to gently scour
All the thoughts that plague your mind
We will clean this temple, fine
Helping you to see divine
To recognize your own design

The outside world, it hurts to watch
That good place, to see it caught
Ensnared in what's a spider's web
But we say time does flow and ebb
And what might seem a dark Earth spell
Will meet its end, all will be well

This a promise of a kind
That you don't easily find
But feel it, daughter
Oh, such peace
To be felt by all, so sweet
Peace of mind is what they call it
This our hope that will befall it

Peace of mind, not war and battle
True peace and for those, the 'cattle'
Good shepherds will guide them well
And ably lead them out of hell
The masses of your people there
Have got themselves in quite a snare
The sooner they become aware

The sooner they can climb the stairs
That lead them to a new affair

So while they've poisoned outer planes
Beneath the ground we've rearranged
And we continue stirring soil
This, we think's a worthy toil
And when good soil is stirred on Earth
It will produce a stirring birth

You, wishing peace in time of war
We will say that outworn whore
Will be laid to rest here soon
We declare on this full Moon

Our declaration we do speak
We don't yell and shout and shriek
No, with the voice of woman here
We say this birth is naught to fear

Opening doors of good hearts, wise
Clearing dust out of their eyes
Attic windows opening
Bringing sunshine, we're hoping

Lighting up the darkest places
Where one sees that friendly faces
Live there too, we hold your hand
Good folk from a distant land

Rescue mission if you will
We will stay with you until
Your temple's cleaned
Your soil is fertile
We'll unlock the serpent's girdle
So you all can once more breathe

And in your minds you will conceive
A place of beauty, we repeat
But it's important that you greet
The face of beauty with respect
When you do you will connect

But this connection, this one's true
It's one that lives inside of you
A mystery of prisms, vast
You will raise this vessel's mast
With what we'd call integrity
You don't believe it but you see
Your heart's in the right place, we say
Mistakes will happen anyway
And so, you've wisened up yourself
Making proud, good Fae and Elf

It's curious how we're ignored
And now Earth's children, they get bored
If not ensnared in their device
For they are caught like wretched mice

But we will not give up on you
Good children of the Earth, so few
Among your folk, with eyes that see
And yet more waking presently

Calling you to steer the ship
That sails on waters that are calm
We call it a healing balm
But see how it rhymes with that? (bomb)
They play with you like a cat
Preying on the little ones
The way some cats do for fun

Take good care of precious soil

Good daughter who always toils
Your body's tired, precious one
Time to have a little fun

And know that success comes to you
You will have more than a few
Of those dollars in your bank
You'll be rising in the rank

Ah dear, please do laugh with us
We don't cause injurious
Effects upon you that we see
Your good soil, no injury
But we'd say it needs energy
So as you gas up your white car
We will give you in this hour
A good injection, energy
So your vessel will be free
Resonating with the Fae
This station is far away

Holding you in poetry
Opening third eye to see
You'll have control of the wheel
Those who torment, they will heel
For it's a game of words they play
But we can best that, we the Fae

In whatever language used
We can come in and infuse
A kind of oil change for your car
Helping you navigate the hour

In your vessel that is bright
You drive in a car that's white
Belonging to a prior age (1998 Camry)

Before they rearranged the stage (911)

Playing metaphors with you
As you know we like to do
Your car is a '98
A 17, a starry gate

Fun to think, a gate that walks
A gate that loves and likes to talk
An open gate for love and truth
We, the folk of perpetual youth
Playing with those words of yours
Helping you to laugh at chores
Some levity we bring to you
This gate has been much abused

Imagine that, abandoned gate
That for so long, none knew its fate
A long-forgotten gate of old
But oh, great stories have been told
In languages too many to count
For this is an infinite fount
Of life force living wondrous, here
Life force giving birth to years
Of multitudes, diversified
Most of which prefer to hide
But living, thriving just the same
The mind of beauty, far from plain
And yet its many planes survive
And they will do more than just thrive

Casting spell on Scorpio Moon
Casting light upon the gloom
Demons shown for what they are
And cast out finally at this hour
Easing suffering at last

A spell of kindness we will cast

So many good people out there
They will soon become aware
Old spells will break everywhere
From that net they'll be unsnared

Away from needless fighting there
To join a greater fight that bears
The fruit that heals, its nectar sweet
It provides more than a treat

Healing Earth, our family
Its good people, they will see
Its good creatures, they will be
Finally living peacefully

The vicious spells that they are casting
They will not be everlasting
They have missed the mark again
And this beleaguered earthly plane
Will not suffer endlessly
Nature works tirelessly
To overcome the wicked schemes
Put forth by those with lofty dreams
Of all the money they will make
They do not care what's at stake

No, to vulgar spells of men
Who think they wield with golden pen
Many statues with their 'clause'
Oh, we recognize those jaws!

Even though they've planned the fall
We say that it won't work at all
We, the shimmering ones of light

Understand this is a fight
A noble fight that's ancient, old
A battle fought hard by the bold

In many ways this battle's fought
In many ways your folk are fraught
With endless problems, endless toil
Yet, with clear mind they can foil
The well-laid plans made quietly
To undermine those who are free

We are helping you to see
To clear you mind so wise ones, we
The Shining People of the Sidhe
With whom you're speaking directly
Can get under your skin at last
And use the lessons of your past
To guide you from experience
That wisdom gleaned will influence
Decisions you'll in future make
So your actions you won't forsake

And on Ireland's emerald shores
For you we'll open other doors
Your good people, we will welcome
We the Faerie and the Elfin
We know those good hearts do seek
And would like more than a peek
Into the magic that we hold
We keep it dear and sometimes, bold
We give away a little gift
That will beguile you with some thrift

Earthly one, we're waking you
Untroubling minds, more than a few
We're dancing here, playing with you

Oh, Faerie sister, it's full Moon
And tonight we are in rare form
Playing with you in your dorm

More are waking in this place
Hallowed soil you can't erase
Good folk rising everywhere
Waking from the sorcerer's snare

We, the people of the Sidhe
We have worked tirelessly
Helping those with eyes to see
To open hearts to wise ones, we
Who'll turn this good Earth, this good garden
Helping those whose hearts have hardened
Helping those good folk to wake
And the sorcerer's spell to break

They tell you that it can't be done
We say, get ready for some fun
That good kitty lying there
Even that cat is aware
And basks with us on this full Moon
Illuminating the night's gloom

We the folk, of Faerie mound
The Elfin people who did found
We who live on hallowed ground
Breaking spells, we promised here
We will say, you've naught to fear
The people of the Sidhe are here

The Elfin kindreds you hold dear
Remember in your Catholic school?
With their dogma and their rules?
They caught you whispering, called you out

Asking all your friends about
Any stories they might hold
About the Faerie folk of old?

You're like a daughter, well, you know
We have watched you ably grow
You, adopted by kind folk
Who reared you well, we did invoke
Most gracious keepers of your soul
To help you steer your vessel, bold
So be kind to your aging mother
That week with her will be like no other

And with those siblings take great care
They too, in waters that they bear
Their own weight on them, daughter, wise
You must see with compassionate eyes

Do not so easily dismiss them
Do not abuse your position
Dear, use that heart you have with care
For opportunity's everywhere
To cast those darts you like to use
We'll say though dear, you've much improved...

YOUR AIM!!!

(Laughing)

Ha! We play with you!
Let us laugh and stay with you
For just another hour or two
So you'll cheer up and not be blue

Daughter, we declare this night
That you, with your second sight

Will see ahead of what will come
And you'll be ready for that one

For your life's changing, get thee ready
Get that good ship strong and steady
You'll be crossing many channels
As you lie there in your flannels

Get the rest your body needs
Then go outside and plant your seeds...

Mushroom Message (September 2021)

Good rest, good daughter, take the gift
Know that you are in a shift
We have got you on a wave
A soft and gentle one He gave
To all of us who called him thus
To cut the boil and drain the pus
And that is what is happening now
Though you cannot figure how
The suffering will help at all
And we hear your sincere call

Now as the Sun is warming you
And the mushroom it imbues
Wisdom to your conscious mind
So you won't be left behind

We are leading you with care
We are with you everywhere
We won't leave you in despair
Or let you get into a snare

Your mind's a free zone, guard it well
In that place they cannot dwell
Keep it clean, dear, thar she blows
Wind to steer you where you go

You will sail right through this mess
And we know of the distress
We will help the others too
The innocents, their hearts are true

When you steer your ship in water
We will help you, blessed daughter
Sometimes waves will make a chop

And you simply cannot stop

You must steer sure and sight your ship
To the horizon where you'll flip
The ancient coin of destiny
Then and there you'll ably see
Where it lands is what will be

Yes, we're playing words with thee
Your eyes open, you can see
And darling, wisdom isn't free
It sure ain't no shopping spree

Cycles come and then they go
Some are quick and some are slow
Some lose steam before they start
And we invite your blessed heart
To hold that one, that vision there
You will charge that well with care...

Mushroom Journey, Faerie Queen and Fates (2021)

Here you are in your cocoon
You will be emerging soon
We will keep you nice and warm
And ensure you don't come to harm

We, the beings of the soil
Appreciate your careful toil
Yes, we know our sounds are strange
In the soil we rearrange

You have called us here today
And we answer, we, the Fae
They can't harm us, daughter, dear
Though you do go into fear
But we tell you, daughter, true
Throughout time we are with you

We are the Faerie of this Earth
And we are ready for Earth's birth
A new time in the constellation
It will change in every nation
What is felt upon your Earth
Is a very difficult birth
What you all must understand
Is we are here to lend a hand
Most of you will turn away
But some of you will stand and stay

This good planet is your home
And dear ones, you're not alone
No, we watch you night and day
We are with you, we, the Fae
We don't simply fade away
Even when the skies look gray

We are in each of you now
Teaching your good spirits how
To activate what is within
This, the time you must begin

We, the good folk of the Earth
We have waited for this birth
The attempts to quell our light
Will go down with quite a fight
Daughter, do not worry so
In your heart you hold the glow
We call you, 'Daughter Who Knows'
That a name we do bestow
Daughter, trust this avenue
You've chose the one we want you to...

Me:
What of my body can you say?
Will this arthritis go away?
What will be the very best?
I am here at your behest
Good ones, wise, tell me today
I will listen to the Fae

Faerie Queen:
Yes, your hands are very cold
You need more blood there, daughter, bold
Use our words to help you well
And that water from your well
Run it through the filters there
Charge it daughter, well, with care

We are teaching you old things
People of the Faerie rings
Bring you to the ancient magic
Keep away from all the tragic

Nonsense that your people say
Daughter, you must stay away

We, the old ones of this Earth
Called you here now for this birth
It's a big one, you won't miss it
Yes, this good Earth, you will kiss it
It ensures you've everything
Including those golden rings
Daughter who savors all life's gifts
We deliver you a lift

Playing with words, as you know
These are seeds we like to sow
And so dear Daughter Who Knows
Your life here will shine and glow
This, you see is a frequency
And this one keeps your good mind free
That's the zone that we do keep
Though the many are asleep
The waking ones will take the reigns
They will break free from their chains

This, an old spell you will break
Those who've cast it will forsake
An abuse of knowledge, old
They've taken the stories told
And twist and turned them into poison
Making messes, lots of noise and
Harnessing the power of mind
That is what they get to bind

And so we call to all who think
The open-eyed ones who don't drink
From that river that is poisoned
No, good daughter, we are poised though

Here and waiting for the call
And when it comes then one and all
Will awaken from this spell
That has made this good place hell

You, good daughter, wish to know
When, old friends, will those seeds grow?
We tell you, daughter, this is new
This age is a different brew
We, who tend your cauldron, old
Daughter, our hearts are not cold
We breathe into you wisdom, dear
Helping you, the path to clear

They are felling all the trees
They are killing many bees
A good mess they are making here
Daughter, they're in a lot of fear
Trying to protect themselves (laughing)
From the beings you call elves

Dear, the keepers of the ages
We, the ones you call the sages
We're entrusted with this place
And yes, they are a different race
They don't understand this place
They will leave here in disgrace
Part of you, dear, knows that's true
So your good heart we imbue

Let the fear and worry go
And just like that water flows
Let the wisdom carry you
To a place where hearts are true
Daughter, we will bring the showers
Your spring will bear many flowers...

Me:
This good body is here still
Next to the well of your good will...

Faerie Queen:
Give it rest and also herbs
Roadside ones found by the curbs
Nettles are a gracious friend
'Twill give you strength till very end
Yes, you've planted all those seeds
They'll deliver you good deeds

What most people consider weeds
Will carry you like noble steeds
The good weeds bow, saluting you
They will take care of the few
Aches and pains that now plague you
We can eradicate those few

Keep planting, daughter, drop those seeds
They will tend to all your needs
Making sure you plant the ones
That will deliver the good fun
Comfrey calls you, it will heal
Daughter, put it where you kneel
On those knees and aching hands
Wrap it round you like a band
Those good leaves know what to do
They will dim what does abuse

And of course, those blessed bees
With their sting, dear, they will free
All the medicine they hold
You partake of it, daughter, bold
You will steward them with care
The good folk who fly in the air

You love to watch them fly and land
And in return they lend their hand
An ancient innocence they hold
It's in you as well, daughter, bold
You are waking from the spell
We will keep your body well...

You will come up in your mind
With the answer to unbind
The evil ruse you must unwind
We'll help you, the way to find
You want a world of grace and beauty?
Kindness is your only duty

Me:
Wait a minute—are you telling me we must be kind?
They are destroying us. Please! Nature spirits, what to do?

Faerie Queen:
They have turned the common flu
Into a thing of mass destruction
They do this by spell's induction

Me:
So how do we defeat the spell?
Not to be impatient but please tell

Faerie Queen:
So many good folk caught in net
The consequence when one forgets

It's the nature of the spider
She devours what sits beside her
And you see they've copied even her
And look at that—made quite a stir
They've got so many in their 'net'

A sticky one, makes you forget

But their nectar isn't sweet
It's the trick and not the treat
You see, when minds get steered away
And they forget how to play
They instead become the prey
Those predators don't go away

Once again, a lesson, large
This one, dear, for those in charge
They're about to eat their words
All those spells that you have heard
We assure you, this birth will be
It will cleanse this Earth and sea
Your good folk will be well
In the end they'll live to tell

The Fates:
Though you fear, oh daughter
We tell you now
Connect to us,
And let the forces drain the pus
It's not pretty, dear, we know
And we feel your heart's sorrow
We, the fates, have made our choice
And daughter, you will have a voice
But death comes first
And then the birth
That is how it is on Earth

Do not worry, daughter dear
As you cry all of those tears
This is what it is to see
But it is how we have to free
Let that *'virus'* have its way

It will only last a day
In time, this is nothing dear
You can see, your eyes are clear
We see you holding to the beauty
It's what you do, it is your duty
More will join you, they will come
Awakening with the bright Sun...

Faerie Queen:
We do see your gentle heart
And good daughter, we impart
Rhyme and reason to your mind
We've ensured that you will find
Your way through their awful spell
And you create dear, very well

Let go those tears, dear
Be sublime
Life is sweet, it's gifts most fine
They place fear into your mind
Those are ideas that you grind
Into flour that you bake
To produce a poison cake
You see daughter, your good mind
It is a master design
Let those thoughts now realign

You know dear, what you must do
Let the sugar go, it's true
We told you once, we'll say again
Let it go, it is a strain
Upon the good Earth of this body
This is more than being naughty
This is part, dear, of their spell
To make your good body unwell
Daughter, lies we do not tell

You will break free of that spell
This good body has more years
It's still a good ship you can steer

Waters coming of great beauty
Ride them well dear, that's your duty
Your grandchildren, they will come
Newborn daughters of the Sun
You will see them, every one
And we, the Fae, will have some fun
They'll partake, they will feel joy
This good place won't be destroyed
You knew well to come here, daughter
You have learned what we have taught here
More joy coming soon to you
Another heart that we imbue
It is time for both of you

You are a good woman, wise
A daughter who can see with eyes
We are cleansing all the ills
Just relax and wait until
Our good medicine is over
Then go out and feel the clover
Cooling to the souls of feet
This good Earth is very sweet... .

Council of the Wise Ones (January 2022)

At the start of this journey, I felt myself at a train station in heavy mist and it seemed to be taking an awfully long time for the train to come. Then, of course, the Sidhe arrived. I later read that the Sidhe would often come through the mist. And at the end of this journey they gave a wink to the theme of the train.

Daughter, to yourself, be kind
We see worry in your mind
We see fretting and regret
That dear, is a sticky net

You know you cannot change the past
To sail ships takes experience vast
Accomplishments and mistakes too
All that lives inside of you
That is quite the cauldron's brew
It does inform and also stews
Daughter, you must pick and choose
Carefully, what you hold and lose

Ride that wave you see so clearly
We will hold it for you, dearly
You will walk this year with Grace
With every step you'll see her face

Daughter, look around you now
It's hard to imagine how
But this weaving just wove itself
That is the magic of the Elf
Magic they don't want you to see
And so they've changed the scenery
But we are always just below
And what we carry, so few know

To certain ones we do bestow
The knowledge of how good seeds grow...

A gentle journey, today's ride
We'll hold you fast while we're inside
We are around you and below
Just call to us and we'll bestow
The ways in which to stay in flow
And ensure that awareness grows

We'll help you get out of their system
We'll say it's about to fall
You are finding the true wisdom
It is clear you've heard the call

Forces strong will see you through
We'll help you with all that you do
This is how much we love you
You still cannot believe it's true
That's quite the spell they've cast on you

It will unbind, 'twill do so soon
That is why at this dark Moon
We come in with greatest stealth
To ensure you regain health
For this next passage you won't miss
And you will seal it with a kiss...

We share with you at this time
So much we'll tell you through this rhyme
The wise old ones who run this place
Know well when it's time to face
The music so your ship, you'll clean
Ready, set for the next scene
Upon this great stage they call Earth
For this new scene's about a birth

The dark old wizards tried to quell
By poisoning the ancient well

But daughter, know, we studied longer
In that college we grew stronger
We've the antidote for that
'Twill cause them all to more than scat
Like that word, dear? Thought you might
They will go down with a fight
You know they underestimate
The ancient ones with wisdom great

And so, this is their last card
And they are working very hard
The human race, they wish to snuff
But their efforts aren't enough

They underestimate the ancient college
That beauty place of sacred knowledge
They thought they could just drop out
And that somehow gives them clout

And they have knowledge, yes, it's true
But what they have cannot construe
The living world of truth and light
All they do is create fright

And so, this winter won't last long
And we've got you where you belong
And we are tending well, your weave
A golden one that you'll conceive

And many hands will help you, dear
And what you spin will be quite clear
A tapestry, a weave so fine
The Muse within is just divine

You came here to spin that one
We promise, dear, this will be fun
And many kindreds, they will come
And add their threads beneath the Sun

This, a birth they cannot quell
This one comes forth from the well
The well that's guarded by the Sidhe
Tended well, by wise ones, we

We've told you daughter, it's the timing
Here we are again, we're rhyming
You won't have to wait that long
Before the Earth bursts forth in song

The spring is an awakening, see?
A metaphor we think will please

You will get the rhythm, dear
Of these rhymes and ship you steer
We will get it through your head
That is why you are in bed

The only way we can reach you
And so, you're here and we'll teach you
You must know, daughter, you are loved
By friends below and too, above
Dear, that is an old injury
You thought you were cast out to sea
All of it, dear, had to be
And now you're with the Good Folk, we
We know that your heart is good
That's why we're in your neighborhood
Don't be so hard on yourself
We surround you, Fae and Elf

That old spell, we wish to break
And witness, you, a new life make
So daughter, you'll unweave this knot
We are here to help you spot
The complication, and resolve
We'll help you easily dissolve
This is your ship and it's a beauty
Steer it well, that is your duty
And daughter, we ride with you now
We are with you at the bow
And you've a scope through which you see
You'll avert storms easily

You've called to you the Old Ones, wise
We do not wear a disguise
We imbue when time is right
We know the weight of this fight

This is why the books of old
Ensured that the stories told
Would seed the minds and set the stage
To bring rightly a new age
One that cannot be infected
We're immune though they've directed
All of their artillery
But it's too late, good seers see
And of a sudden, minds are free

They tell you it can't be done
They're trying to quell the Sun
They know well, the time's begun
And the poison they have spun
Will be unbound by clever hands
True graduates, the Shining Band
Of wise and kindly kindreds, dear
Don't think we don't know how to clear

This, the lesson that they missed
They left early—class dismissed
We stayed longer, got the spell
We know how to transform hell
Into a wondrous place of beauty
We maintain that it's our duty

We will right what's torn asunder
We will heal what they have plundered
We're what you call 'clean-up crew'
The experts that know what to do
You wonder why we talk to you
Daughter, you doubt your own value

Hear us now, that spell must break
You will do all that it takes
Not easy but you've got this one
You have good teachers, we're the ones
And we'll ensure you'll learn this lesson
For you dear, school's still in session
Let us gently filter in
Threads to create a different spin

So daughter, feed the ones with ears
Help them know that they can steer
Their vessels to a place that's calm
Where they can find the healing balm

That balm is a different brew
Not the kind that sorcerers blew
This one dear, spelled with an 'L'
This balm makes all of you well

ME:
How can we help these poor lost people?
In their minds they've become sheeple

It's not right to hack the mind
It's unjust and most unkind

Let us build a frequency
That helps the blind begin to see
Please, let's help them realize
And recognize the thin disguise

Of rulers who pretend to care
While holding Earth within a snare
The beauty here they want to steal
They wish to make our people kneel
To those dark masters who cause strife
And seek to control all of life

And so good Fellowship of Light
Ancient ones who come when night
Is darkest, when so few can see
I call humbly to thee
Lead my people into reason
Expose our leaders for their treason

Unhook their talons from this place
What they have done is a disgrace
Remove them please, do what is needed
Help the wisdom to be seeded

Council of the Wise Ones, there
Please have ears for the despair
I know your wisdom's helped before
Let us give the lost an oar
And a map that they can see
To get them out of misery
A lamp to help them find their way
Through and beyond the wretched fray

Let us weave fabric of light
Illuminating this dark night
The blind aided by those of sight
We will help their ships to right

Dear Council of the Wise and Free
Please give Earth's people eyes to see
So many of them are good souls
And they deserve to become whole

So, like a lawyer, I intervene
For what I see is just obscene
And so, with humble heart I ask
I know that this is quite the task

Good folk here stripped in evil ways
And I can see how they're displayed
What passage is this we must ride?
How ever will we get our stride?

I call a very special weave
One that the sorcerers won't conceive
With humbleness I ask you, please
To bring an end to cough and sneeze
It's quite the spell that they have spun
I know that they have just begun

ANSWER FROM THE FAE:
Well, things can end quite suddenly
Next thing you know you stand there free
A whole new world beneath your feet
New possibilities to greet

And so dear, trust the Old Ones, wise
Of course, we can hear well, your cries
Don't think we know not what to do

We are expanded through and through

Ages turn like sturdy wheels
So, understand at times it feels
Like doom's upon you, dark with death
Just when you think it's your last breath
Then suddenly the fire's stoked
And that light that you invoked
Arrived in time to greet the day
To cast the dark winged ones away

Trust in the fates, Daughter Who Knows
All those worries, to and fro
It's now time to let them go
The seeds are planted, they will grow
They're in you and many more
We'll only say that what's in store
Will defy any spell they cast
They underestimate the vast
Proportions of this earthly dwelling
This land that they think they're selling...
Daughter, know, good seeds we sow
And at this time, they'll ably grow
It may not seem so in your eyes
The best spells dear, are a surprise
This is a 'game', we'll use that word
Though really dear, it's quite absurd

We'll say it's old, but that's not right
For that would make it seem so trite
Just know, daughter, that you're a player
As your girls would say, a 'slayer'

You will weave a web of gold
And daughter, what that web will hold
And you are not the only weaver

As you know, many conceivers

As they say, it's two or more
Who can create what is in store
And so, a new year's upon you
And this one brings a mighty brew
That will revive more than a few
To fight for what is right and true

For what's to be and what will come
Will ensure that the spell's undone
And more will recognize as false
The ones in charge who have no pulse

Daughter, this passage will be short
It will not be your escort
Many folk will come to see
Then you'll create what is to be

We do not chastise, daughter, dear
We simply help your ship to steer
We say you have nothing to fear
We have insured that help is near

We have arranged a life for you
While so many good folk fear the flu
In your nest, good daughter, you
Are weaving spells that you construe
That help the many wake from sleep
And this is why your brew must steep

This is done when minds are clear
The only way that you can steer
We know that they've clouded the mind
And we can see what stands behind
The curtain on their stage of woe

They represent a mighty foe

At some point though, a dam must break
And those who've caused it will forsake
What's been withheld will erupt
And overtake all the corrupt
Creations those dark ones have wrought
When that dam breaks, they just cannot
Prevent that flow of information
'Twill be known by every nation
True knowledge will save the day
And reason will again hold sway

We know that you seek wisdom here
We will help your ship to steer
We are the Good Folk, we are here
In your mind we come and clear
The detritus, the old spent wood...

So daughter dear, you caught the train
Or it caught you and our refrain
Is trust the choreography
And spend more time beneath the trees
And know that we're always with you
And we will give more than a clue
In fact, we'll make it obvious
And more good minds will then discuss
The many possibilities
Of what can be when minds are free...

Sound Advice: Mushroom Journey (September 2023)

And so today a different story
In we come in all our glory
Reluctantly, you always come
Only to find that you have fun

We stand by you, day and night
And when you go into fright
We try to chase those fears away
But we cannot always slay
That dragon you have in your mind
It is the unruly kind

Another place you need to mend
So when your life turns round that bend
You'll be firm and stand there, steady
Even when your life gets heady

Many changes soon to come
You're about to meet the one
You've thought about for all these years
In he comes now, crystal clear

We will tell you even more
We can see what is in store
All those fears you have in there
Turn your mind into a snare

You'll be safe while we're inside
This will be a gentle ride
Here with you again we are
Just call us, we're never far
You can do this life of yours
This next chapter opens doors
We know you're hard on yourself

We will guide you, Fae and Elf

Your mind chatter, it must end
This, the message that we send
Those thoughts contribute oh so much
The bad thoughts get you in a clutch

Instead of seeing through your fear
Investigate ways that are clear
That open pathways you can walk
'Twill be a more productive talk
Stay right here, the road is clear
You make yourself sick with that fear

We come inside you for a time
And hopefully 'twill be sublime
You come to us for wisdom's light
And to ease some of that fright

Like a disease it grips you
But daughter, *see* it's just a brew
You can easily let that go
In place of that, dear, you must know

You are here to live and grow
And to you we ably bestow
A chapter that you will hold dear
But you must let go of that fear

Use the power in your mind
And to this body please be kind
It has served you all this time
Heed the wisdom in this rhyme
Your body's asking for a break
At this age there is more at stake
You do good things for this body

And in other ways you're naughty
Balance is what we advise
That is coming from the wise

If you stray from Nature's laws
You'll be held within the claws
Of demon dragons that will cause
Punishment for broken laws

And so, this message that we speak
Is meant for strong as well as meek
Nature's laws are in your body
That is why you can't be naughty
Your body will tell on you
It knows what you're supposed to do
These laws aren't meant to torment you
But this is why the wise are few

Law extends everywhere you look
It's a very ancient book
Written in the skies for you
Those who study are imbued
With understanding and with might
Its knowledge gives those good wings flight

This is law that you aren't taught
What is poison, what is not
Mistakes are made that help you learn
That is why wisdom is earned
And for some, the same mistake
Over and over the coals are raked

That sad drug they put everywhere
Sugar, causes much despair
Stripped of all Nature's attire
It creates a mighty fire

Not one of life, but one of death
It has shortened many breaths
This is sobering, we know
But you have much more here to grow

It is with love that we deliver
This arrow belongs in your quiver
Nature's laws will sort it out
Those laws are the ones with clout

Of course, we'll help you, daughter, dear
Lean on us, we're always near
We tend to this ancient seer
Let us make your pathway clear

Shadow hides all that is hidden
That is where what is forbidden
Thrives in secret revelry
Hidden from the cavalry

Those shadow beasts are in your gut
And with their teeth they like to cut
Upon the sugared things you eat
You're feeding them with all that's sweet

Deep, they live within the bowels
Living off you with their scowls
They are wreaking havoc there
This will lead to much despair

And so dear, Nature speaks to you
In a pressing way, and you
Must attend to your good ship
This bad habit, you will nip

Drink your broth and eat your kraut

Coax those little monsters out
For they prefer the sticky sweet
That festers with your stomach's heat
A toxic brew's created there
That spreads its ferment everywhere

And so these words convey a warning
And we know it sounds alarming
Your discipline, it must extend
To what you eat so that you end
A cycle, long, that's run its course
We offer you a different horse
To take you on a path of health
That is the true measure of wealth

Hopefully, our voices heard
And you will end all this absurd
Behavior that is beneath you
You have a lovely cauldron's brew
We want to see a healthy stew

And so that demon you will slay
And you will do this the right way
That honors the Creator's grace
'Twill put a smile upon His face

For dear, He wants the best for you
And so you'll step into a new
Life that calls you to its side
Of Nature's laws you will abide

Guidance comes from Nature's laws
How not to fall into the claws
Of hungry demons who will eat
Everything they see as sweet

Yes dear, that is our message, clear
Fix that one and you will steer
Yourself into waters, clear
It only takes a week or two
To end those cravings that plague you

And in your worldly dealings there
Make sure to keep yourself aware
Important that you've eyes to see
That will keep your good mind free
Be vigilant in all you do
And with care you will construe
A way of life you came to live
Take the advice that we give

Keep your vision crystal clear
And keep our counsel ever near
Then you will know what to do
This time you're in you will get through

This a time of many choices
Out there in a sea of voices
Discernment needed at this time
If exercised then you'll be fine

In those choices that you make
Think with clear head, see the snake
Deception's everywhere you look
Propaganda is the hook

You find yourself on land that's new
Look with care for any clue
That warns or offers helpful ways
To navigate the sorcerer's maze

Even if the many can't
And the wisdom there is scant
Your connection's sure and strong
It will guide you well along

This path of learning that you walk
You do more than simply talk
Aries woman, Leo heart
Ascendant, Virgo, a good start

You've tempered along the way
Still, your sword, it ably slays
Wield with care and do your best
Deliver wisdom from your nest

You're here to bring that to the many
Daughter, you can handle any
Challenge there that might arise
You've been gifted seer's eyes

Life and love cannot be quelled
They'll pay for everyone they've felled
Just know, daughter, you are held
In loving arms and you, a meld
Created by a great high master
Your life won't end in disaster

You're created for a reason
Live it up, dear, it's your season
More good fortune coming soon
Your good heart is going to swoon

Get that body good and ready
You'll need your feet, dear, to stand steady
You have worked hard for this one
It's time to have a little fun

Those young homemakers, you admire
Kindle in you a gentle fire
No, you can't relive the past
But you can nurture love that lasts
And welcome grandchildren to you
As precious as the morning dew

Even though the world's a mess
Assuage some of that distress
Equilibrium's your friend
Maintain that till very end
Your good mind's taken you this far
Always seeking, yes you are

We have been assigned to you
We help you with that cauldron's brew
Feed your mind and learn the law
Nature's creed beheld with awe
You'll be inspired and you'll write
You will grow your second sight

Keep that mind clear, calm and steady
Your wisdom will reach the ready
The truth will come to more and more
It's unlocked and dear, that door
Will open all the way it can
It's one that they can't easily ban

They can't, for truth is like a light
And that is what conquers the night
Dear, truth is what will put to right
The darkness of your nation's plight

You want a message from the wise?
Deliver truth to those with eyes
And ears that hear and recognize
That stops evil in disguise

Truth will lead you out of hell
Truth will keep you very well
Nature has laws for a reason
And they dictate every season...

The Real Estate (2023)

Despite the troubles in this world
Despite the evil they have hurled
Despite their techniques they're proud of
They can't destroy the sacred dove

They would claim it as their own
They sow desire for that throne
But they cannot touch that seat
It can't be taken by great feats

It's in a place that they can't enter
This, the home of ancient mentors
This, the place of wisdom's light
This, a fire that burns bright

All who come with heart of gold
Will be greeted by the old
Mentors of the ages, past
Who hold with care, the knowledge, vast

This place, they cannot destroy
It's found in every girl and boy
And man and woman of this Earth
Its light shines in every birth

Found within if humbly sought
This is why they just cannot
Effectively put out its light
Regardless of their daunting might

Truth will win out in the end
In spite of how the darkness bends
And twists and perverts endlessly
Yet Truth prevails, 'twill set you free

The wicked cannot take that throne
Lies and deceit are all they've known
It can't be bartered, bought or sold
It can't be stolen by the bold

This, a code they cannot break
This, a riddle they can't make
Into a formula to sell
Entry's barred to those who dwell
Within the realm of greed and hate

This throne is the real estate...

Endnotes

1 "Working with the Angels: The Young Child and the Spiritual World," published by WECAN.

2 https://www.sophiamundi.vic.edu.au/fairy-tales-healing-food-for-the-childs-soul-waldorf-education-steiner-education-alternative-education/

3 *The Woman in the Shaman's Body*, Barbara Tedlock, PhD, Bantam Books, 2005.

4 *A God Who Makes Fire: The Bardic Mysticism of Amergin*, Christopher Scott Thompson, 2013.

5 *Time Stands Still: New Light on Megalithic Science*, Keith Critchlow, Brécourt Academic, 2nd edition, December 31, 2007.

6 *The Elements of the Celtic Tradition*, Caitlin Matthews, Element Books Ltd., 1989.

7 Cormac mac Cuilennáin, *Sanas Chormaic*, N.1231, p.160.

8 Unknown, Imcallam in dá Thuarad, v. 9, *The Bird Cloaks of Ireland: An Investigation of the Tuigen* by Sianluc A. M. Heart.

9 *Rigveda*, IX, 86, 24.

10 *Drunk the Night Before* by Marty Roth, Univ Of Minnesota Press; First Edition July 1, 2008.

11 *The Elements of the Celtic Tradition*.

12 *British Fairy Origins*, Lewis Spence, The Aquarian Press; New edition, January 1, 1981.

13 *The Fairy Mythology* by Thomas Keightley, London, William Harrison Ainsworth, 1850.

14 *European Mythology* by Jacqueline Simpson Peter Bedrick Books; 1998 edition January 1, 1987.

15 *The Fairy Faith in Celtic Countries*, W. Y. Evans-Wentz, Citadel Press, Reprint Edition, January 1, 1994.

16 Ibid.

17 *Fairy Haunts of Ireland*, Alanna Moore, Python Press, 2023.

18 Quoted in An *Encyclopedia of Fairies*, Katharine Briggs, The Pantheon and Fairy Tale Folklore Library, 1976.

19 *An Encyclopedia of Fairies*.

20 Ibid.

21 *Touchstones for Today*, Alanna Moore, Python Press, Australia, 2013 Edition.

22 *The Vanishing People*, Katharine Briggs, Pantheon Books New York, 1978.

23 *Studies in Scottish Literature*, Volume 33, Issue 1, Article 27, "Ballads and the Supernatural: Spells, Channs, Curses and Enchantments," Sheila Douglas, 2004.

24 https://www.youtube.com/watch?v=6zZy2Q3QY0Q

25 *The Secret Country*, Janet and Colin Bord, Warner Books Edition, 1976.

26 *The Fairy Mythology*, Thomas Keightley, 1828.

27 *Ploughing the Clouds: The Search for Irish Soma*, Peter Lamborn Wilson, City Lights Publishers; First Edition, January 1, 2001.

28 "The Mead of Inspiration," Christian Ratsch, Ph.D., in *Tyr: Myth, Culture, Tradition*, Vol. 4, Pub. 2014.

29 *The Encyclopaedia of Celtic Wisdom*, Caitlin and John Matthews, Element Books, Ltd. 1994.

30 *Celtic Visions: Seership, Omens and Dreams of the Otherworld*, by Caitlin Matthews, Watkins Publishing London, 2012.

31 *The Earth Spirit: Its Ways Shrines and Mysteries*, John Michell, The Crossroad Publishing Company, 1975.

32 *Courting the Wild Queen*, Seán Pádraig O'Donoghue, Ritona Press, 2022.

33 Michell, *The Earth Spirit*.

34 *Secrets of the Stones*, John Michell, Inner Traditions International, Ltd, 1989.

35 Ibid.

36 *Touchstones for Today*, Alanna Moore.

37 *The Earth Spirit*, John Michell.

38 Ibid.

39 *Paramagnetism*, Philip S. Callahan, Ph.D., Acres U.S.A., 1995.

40 Ibid.

41 *The Earth Spirit*, Michell.

42 *The Secret Country*, Janet and Colin Bord, Warner Books Edition, 1976.

43 Ibid.

44 *Witches (RLE Witchcraft): Investigating an Ancient Religion*, First Edition, Part of Routledge Library Editions: Routledge, 2011.

45 *The Secret Country*, Janet and Colin Bord.

46 Ibid.

47 *History of the Kings of Britain*, Geoffrey of Monmouth, Penguin Books; First Edition, 1977.

48 *The Waves That Heal*, Mark Clement, Mokelumne Hill Press, 1963.

49 *The Hidden Ireland: A Study of Gaelic Munster in the Eighteenth Century*, Daniel Corkery, Gill & Macmillan, 1967.

50 Ibid.

51 *Celtic Traditions*, Caitlin Matthews, Watkins Publishing, 2012.

La Ghirlandata, "The Garlanded figure",
Dante Gabriel Rossetti, 1873.

SHONAGH HOME is a teacher, counselor, author and poet. Of Celtic heritage, she follows the wisdom of the ancients, and is inspired by the *Ban Draoi* (dree) and *fili*, (Gaelic for a Celtic medicine woman/seer/poet). As a modern medicine woman, she brings her connection to Nature and the spirit worlds into her flourishing practice, hosting retreats and online counseling sessions, where she works psycho-spiritually with clients from all over the world. She specializes in shadow work, delving into the rich territory of the psyche. Shonagh has studied with master teachers, and for the past 12 years has apprenticed herself to the mushroom teachers who have led her into profound connection with the spirits of Nature and her ancestral roots. She is author of *Ix Chel Wisdom, Love and Spirit Medicine,* and *Poetic Whispers from the Cauldron of the Otherworld.* In addition, she hosts the podcast, The Mushroom's Apprentice.

www.shonaghhome.com